ISBN 978-1-331-94365-5
PIBN 10257789

For support please visit www.forgottenbooks.com

1 MONTH OF
FREE
READING

at

www.ForgottenBooks.com

By purchasing this book you are eligible for one month membership to ForgottenBooks.com, giving you unlimited access to our entire collection of over 700,000 titles via our web site and mobile apps.

To claim your free month visit:

www.forgottenbooks.com/free257789

English
Français
Deutsche
Italiano
Español
Português

www.forgottenbooks.com

Mythology Photography **Fiction**
Fishing Christianity **Art** Cooking
Essays Buddhism Freemasonry
Medicine **Biology** Music **Ancient
Egypt** Evolution Carpentry Physics
Dance Geology **Mathematics** Fitness
Shakespeare **Folklore** Yoga Marketing
Confidence Immortality Biographies
Poetry **Psychology** Witchcraft
Electronics Chemistry History **Law**
Accounting **Philosophy** Anthropology
Alchemy Drama Quantum Mechanics
Atheism Sexual Health **Ancient History**
Entrepreneurship Languages Sport
Paleontology Needlework Islam
Metaphysics Investment Archaeology
Parenting Statistics Criminology
Motivational

GEORGE WESTINGHOUSE

His Life and Achievements

BY

FRANCIS E. LEUPP

Illustrated from Photographs

BOSTON

LITTLE, BROWN, AND COMPANY

1919

20173

Norwood Press

Set up and electrotyped by J. S. Cushing Co., Norwood, Mass., U.S.A.
Presswork by S. J. Parkhill & Co., Boston, Mass., U.S.A.

TO MY DEAR OLD FRIEND
THE HONORABLE MARTIN A. KNAPP,
WHO HAS LABORED FOR THE RAILWAYS
ON THEIR ECONOMIC SIDE
AS GEORGE WESTINGHOUSE DID FOR THEIR
PHYSICAL STRENGTH AND SAFETY

PREFACE

ALTHOUGH George Westinghouse was, in the broadest sense, a public servant, my own acquaintance with him was only social. As he left behind him no diaries, no files of personal correspondence, and scarcely any other sources of supply on which the biographer of a political or military celebrity depends for much interesting material, I have been obliged to rely, in the main, on the memories of the friends of Mr. Westinghouse, local tradition and gossip in neighborhoods where he had lived, the records of courts and minutes of public meetings, corporate reports and partnership account books, old volumes of newspapers and magazines, miscellaneous scrapbooks, and the like. One day, let us hope, we may have from the pen of some well-known expert in technology an adequate summary of what the whole world's industrial advancement owes to the work of the eminent inventor. The mission of the present volume is simply human. It will have been accomplished if it conveys to the young man of today a sense that his career will depend for success less on the splendor of its start than on the spirit in which he pursues it; far less on capital than on courage, on worry than on watchfulness, on "pull" than on persistence.

Of the gentlemen to whom I am indebted for assistance in this task, I beg here to return thanks to Mr. Ernest H. Heinrichs, who for some years was attached to the personal staff in the Westinghouse office in Pittsburgh, and who passed over to me the copious notes he had made with a view to a possible biography of his chief; to Mr. H. C. Tener, the last private secretary of Mr. Westinghouse; to Mr. Alexander G. Uptegraff, who for a long period was a member of the family circle and represented Mrs. Westinghouse in many of her social and charitable projects; to Mr. George W. Jones, a relative who is still engaged in business at the old headquarters of "G. Westinghouse & Co." in Schenectady, New York; to the authors of the excellent books and magazine articles from which I have drawn facts or inspiration; and to a number of interesting men and women whom I have quoted in my narrative. In an effort to avoid errors, I have, as far as practicable, submitted doubtful passages to various persons whose criticism would be valuable, and in all cases where their opinions disagreed I have exercised my own discretion. I am making this statement as a matter of fairness to every one concerned.

F. E. L.

WASHINGTON, D. C.,
   July 1, 1918.

CONTENTS

CHAPTER   PAGE

        PREFACE vii

      I   "AT FIRST, THE INFANT" 1

     II   "THE AGE 'TWIXT BOY AND YOUTH"   13

    III   SOLDIER AND SAILOR, STUDENT AND SWAIN   29

    IV   OPPORTUNITY KNOCKS AT THE DOOR 47

     V   DOUBT CHANGED TO CERTAINTY 62

    VI   "NOTHING SUCCEEDS LIKE SUCCESS" 76

   VII   THE BATTLE OF THE BRAKES 91

  VIII   OPENING A MINE OF GASEOUS WEALTH . . . 106

    IX   WHAT THE GAS DID FOR PITTSBURGH . . . 119

     X   THE CONTEST OF THE CURRENTS 131

    XI   THE STRUGGLE IN NEW YORK 143

   XII   ORIGIN OF THE "STOPPER" LAMP 156

  XIII   FROM NIAGARA TO THE NAVY 171

  XIV   "BLUSHING HONORS THICK UPON HIM" . . . 188

   XV   A SECOND FINANCIAL ORDEAL 204

  XVI   AIR SPRINGS AND ADDRESSES 219

  XVII   A BIG MAN'S HUMAN SIDE 232

XVIII   "THE OLD MAN" AND HIS EMPLOYEES   246

  XIX   A TRIO OF HOMES 259

   XX   INSIGNIA OF CHARACTER 274

  XXI   "LAST SCENE OF ALL" 290

       INDEX 301

LIST OF ILLUSTRATIONS

George Westinghouse   *Frontispiece in Photogravure*

The Mother and Father of George Westinghouse   FACING PAGE

Birthplace at Central Bridge, N. Y.   "   "   10

George Westinghouse. From a War Time Portrait   "   "   30

George Westinghouse and Mrs. Westinghouse
     during their Earlier Days of Wedded Life   "   "   46

The First Westinghouse Air Brake Factory   "   "   72

Locomotive and Passenger Car That Constituted a
     Part of the First Train Used for a Public Ex-
     hibition of the Brake   .   .   .   .   .   "   "   76

"Solitude," the Westinghouse Home at Pittsburgh   "   "   122

Marguerite Erskine Westinghouse   .   .   .   .   "   "   134

George Westinghouse at Work   .   .   .   .   "   "   180

Erskine Manor, the Lenox Residence   "   "   264

GEORGE WESTINGHOUSE

CHAPTER I

"At First, the Infant"

In the northeast corner of Schoharie County, New York, lies the village of Central Bridge. To most travelers on the railroad that skirts its border it is only a way station, to students of the map a dot; but to it our country owes a debt, for out of it came one of those uncommon men whose achievements have shed luster upon the American name in all parts of the earth, and whose character is a precious heritage to younger generations in search of an exemplar. He was not a military hero, though he tasted war; he was not a statesman, though counting Presidents and Kings among his friends; he was master of no magic arts, yet his clever hands, responsive to a fertile mind, were always busy converting prophecy into history. He gloried in the fact that he was simply a man among men, with sturdy muscles and an active brain, whose so-called genius consisted of the broadest of human sympathies and the keenest sense of future possibilities harnessed to a tireless perseverance.

Central Bridge, which is not yet a large community, was in the earlier half of the last century the heart of a back-country farming district.   Its aboriginal possessors were the Mohegan Indians, who opened several trails from the Hudson and Mohawk valleys into the Schoharie valley, and made some primitive efforts at agriculture.   Its first permanent white settlement appears to have been by the German Palatine immigrants after their dispersion from the Livingston Manor.   They arrived in a condition of great poverty, bearing all their worldly goods bound to their shoulders, and endured every kind of discouraging experience while they were making the wilderness habitable.   There was something infectious in their stubborn refusal to be crushed by hardships.   It spread to the new neighbors who gradually moved into the valley, which, though suffering not a little from raids in the war of the Revolution, gradually blossomed forth with fertile and well-tilled farms, and became dotted here and there with churches, schools, mills, and small factories, the latter run by the local water powers.   It is because the resolute spirit of those early days had in it a quality of presage that I have drawn upon them for a background to the opening scenes of my story.

There are now, strictly speaking, two villages of Central Bridge, five minutes' walk apart.   The old Central Bridge of the histories lies in the opening of the V-shaped point made by the junction of Cobleskill Creek with the Schoharie River, and is separated from its modern namesake by the Creek.   The new village has grown up around the station since the railroad was run through the valley. To the old village came, about 1836, one George Westinghouse, bred a farmer, self-trained a mechanic, with a special taste for carpentry. He represented the second generation of the name in this country. Born and reared near North Pownal, Vermont, he had been stirred by what he heard of the newly opened West, and removed soon after his marriage in 1831 to a farm on the banks of the Cuyahoga River in Ohio, not far from Cleveland. The climate, however, did not prove to his liking or to his wife's; so after a rather short stay they returned to the East, settling first at Minaville, in Montgomery County, New York. It is believed to have been there that the bent was given to his mind which shaped his whole after career.

One of his neighbors had acquired a threshing machine, and this, being a novelty thereabout, interested Westinghouse, who soon fell to planning means for improving its efficiency. The subject haunted his thoughts continually, and his leisure moments were often employed with pencil and paper, sketching little designs for parts which he conceived could be remodeled with advantage. His wife encouraged him in this new departure, and warmly approved his suggestion that he might change his occupation and become a maker of machinery. But Minaville, they both felt certain, was no place for a factory of the sort he contemplated : it was far from a base of supplies. He had heard of Central Bridge, with its two abundant water courses, its system of highways radiating in every direction, and its convenient distance from the growing town of Schenectady. A visit of inspection satisfied him that it was the site he was looking for, and he lost no time in making the move.

Too conservative a manager to give up farming till he was entirely assured of the success of his manufacturing experiment, he bought a fair-sized tract of bottom land where the river and the creek meet. Here stood already a few buildings, one of which he expanded into a shop, where he could repair the machinery of a brace of mills that were near by, and work out in wood some of the designs he had sketched.

Before long it became plain that he must choose definitely between his two occupations and devote his attention exclusively to one, and, as a patent he had taken out had begun to bring returns, he made over most of his farm work to hired hands and spent his days at the bench. His mechanical operations gradually outgrew the original shop, and an extension had to be added. This, in its turn, meant more capital and more help, both of which were forthcoming from the neighborhood, where the people had come to recognize in him a man of more than ordinary ability. His inventions included improvements not only in threshing machines, but in winnowing appliances, endless-chain horse powers, and several allied devices, as well as a seed-scraper for broom corn which attracted notice by its ingenuity.

Mrs. Westinghouse, born Emmeline Vedder, was of Dutch-English stock. She was a woman of strong common sense, with a considerable imaginative faculty. Though she knew too little of the mechanic

THE MOTHER AND FATHER OF GEORGE WESTINGHOUSE

arts to enter into her husband's plans in detail, she
had unbounded faith in him, and helped him where
she could. By this time they had six children,
three boys and three girls — healthy, active, noisy
little folk, whom often it was hard to keep from getting under foot in their father's shop.

One autumn evening Mr. Westinghouse came in
looking unusually tired, but with a light in his eye
which his wife interpreted as meaning that he had
caught a glimmer of hope through a tangle of per-
plexities which he had attempted to explain to her
the day before. His thoughts were so immersed in
the subject with which they had been struggling all
day that he almost failed to recognize an elderly
woman from the village who was stirring about in-
doors, and whom he vaguely remembered to have
seen there on one or two former occasions, lending a
hand at the household work and looking after the
children. The supper table was set, and his wife
was in her chair at her accustomed end, but not eat-
ing. She did not rise as he entered, nor did she offer
to assist as the neighbor helped the hungry children
into their places.

The meal was eaten almost in silence. The husband was abstracted in manner, the children were
repressed by the presence of an outsider, the wife was
reticent as became her attitude toward these occasional moods of his, which she knew portended some
development of consequence. When an opening
came she inquired, half timidly:

"Has it been a good day for you?"

"It's too soon to speak positively," he answered,

"but I'm pretty sure I've got that connection to work.　There are two or three things I must figure out still."

"You'll have those by to-morrow night," she said, in the hopeful tone he knew so well.　"I'm glad you're near the end."

"I shall have all the figuring done before I go to bed," he declared.　"I've reached a point now where I couldn't sleep if I tried, and I shan't try."

She made no attempt to argue with him as to the wisdom of his stealing some rest : she knew too well what this manner signified.　As soon as supper was finished she took the children with her to the upper story, while the neighbor rapidly cleared the table, spread it with its colored cover, set the lamp on it, and withdrew.　The man of the house went out to his shop, and presently came back bearing a handful of papers, chiefly rough pencil drawings and scraps covered with mathematical calculations.　These he laid out in a certain order on the table, drew up a chair, and two minutes later was sketching and figuring, and otherwise dead to the world.　His first release from the spell was when the clock struck four. Then he looked up, stretched himself, and with a great sigh of relief blew out the light and lay down on the sofa with his eyes closed.　He felt that he could afford to take a brief recess now, for he had brought the last of his calculations to the desired conclusion, and it would do him good to think them over at his ease, preparatory to laying hold of his tools with the coming of daylight and translating his theoretical results into a concrete piece of machinery.

It was after six o'clock when he reopened his eyes with a start and sat up. The sun was lazily playing on the leaves of a lilac bush that fringed the window. He looked about him, still too stupid with sleep to realize fully where he was or how he chanced to be there. The papers scattered over the table, however, recalled his night's work and reminded him that he must hasten now to the shop. The October morning had a tang of frost in it, and, as the kettle was on the back of the kitchen stove, he made a fire and had a cup of hot coffee to drink with the hasty breakfast for which he foraged while gathering up his litter from the dining room. He tried to tiptoe out of the house, but was arrested by his wife's voice at the head of the stairs, softly calling his name.

"Yes?" he called back, somewhat startled. "What's the matter?"

"Are you going out? You haven't been to bed."

"No, I've been working all night on those drawings and specifications. Can I do anything for you?"

Obviously there was nothing, for a negative was implied in a brief pause; and then —

"What day is this?"

"Tuesday, the sixth. Why?"

"Oh" — with just a shade of hesitancy — "never mind. You won't wait for breakfast?"

"I've had a little — all I need. Don't wait dinner for me; I'll be home as soon as I can drop things."

He felt a slight pang of discomfort at leaving her thus abruptly, for somehow she did not seem quite herself; but this was quickly crowded out by a thought of the shop and the task which awaited him there. The last trace of uncertainty passed with her cheery response:

"Well, good luck to the new invention !"

It was a busy day. The morning sped and noon came, but he forgot dinner and everything else except the job in progress on the bench. The afternoon wore away — one o'clock, two o'clock, three — at last! It was almost four when, the final touches having been given to the working model, he strode out of the shop with the glad step of a prisoner set at liberty. As he approached the cottage he missed the usual sound of the children at play in the yard. Opening the door, he was about to shout upstairs to announce his accomplishment, when he came face to face with the neighbor, who held her finger to her lips.

"Speak low, please," she admonished him. "I've sent the children over to my son's to get rid of their noise. She's been asleep about an hour now. And," noting his look of alarm, "the baby's a boy, and a big one. He came at twenty minutes past eleven. The doctor got here just in time. They're both all right."

The baby! The word fell upon his ear with a sort of shock, like the sudden sound which rouses one from a dream. It was followed by a flood of wonder at his own wooden indifference, as the events of the last twenty-four hours moved in panoramic review through his memory. Of course — here was the explanation of so many things which had made only a shadowy impression on his mind as he noticed them: his wife's comparative inactivity, the uncommon quiet of the house, the presence of the elderly neighbor, the generous, self-effacing thought for him which prevented any suggestion of the nearness of the crisis lest it might distract his mind from the problem on the eve of solution!

He crept stealthily up the stairs to the chamber in which the mother was lying in bed, very still. She had just awakened, and looked up at him with a curious smile playing over her face.

"How does the machine come on?"

"It's finished, and it works."

"Good!"

Her eyes followed him as he gently drew aside the topmost fold of a flannel wrapping that swathed a formless bundle in a crib by the bedside.

"Aren't you pleased that it's a boy?" she whispered.

"I'm glad it's all over, and that you have come through so well," he answered in a noncommittal way, "though I thought you were hoping for a girl."

"I was, at first; but ever since you began this last machine I have had it in my mind night and day — you seemed so wrapped up in it. And then I began to hope we might have another boy, so that he could help you with your work, and in course of time take it up where you leave it. He is born on the very day of your triumph, George, and I want him to be named for you."

In vain the father protested that one George Westinghouse was enough in the family: the mother would listen to no counter proposal. And thus George Westinghouse, Junior, made his bow to the world on the sixth of October, 1846.

The childhood of this latest addition to the family was not distinguished from the life of other lads in the village by anything that seemed to point to the mark he was one day to make in the world. On the contrary, he was noted chiefly for his continual revolt against the confinement of the schoolroom, his distaste for textbooks and routine study, and his pugnacious disposition. He entered more or less into the sports of his schoolmates, but ordinary games did not attract him strongly. The one place in which he would rather be than anywhere else was his father's shop. His father was resolved that he should apply himself to his studies, and used to forbid him the shop during school hours; but George was not inclined to yield to such indirect compulsion, and, if he had made up his mind on a given morning not to go to school, go he would not, but would stubbornly stretch himself on the grass somewhere and play for hours with a few pieces of wood, whittling them into mechanical shapes and pivoting them together with bent pins, so that they would interplay like the jointed members of a piece of machinery. Not a few of the adult villagers used to look upon him with an air of pity, and wonder what was to become of so ill-promising a boy when he grew up.

Discriminating observers might have read in some of his traits which were then regarded as least amiable the signs of a masterful quality. If he felt any specially strong desire, he would not brook the slightest opposition to his efforts to gratify it. When persistent demands were unavailing, he would fly into a rage which was terrifying to behold. Old

Birthplace at Central Bridge, N.Y.

neighbors of the family still remember these parox-
ysms, which took the form first of screaming and
stamping, and then of throwing himself flat and banging his head against any hard surface that came most
convenient — the floor, the wall of a room, the side
of a house. Near the family cottage was a large flat
stone on which he repeatedly thus tried conclusions
with his skull. If every one about him remained
obdurate, he would keep up the disturbance till his
strength was utterly exhausted. Usually, however,
some older member of the household, unable to endure the demonstration longer, would yield the point
at issue, and his tears, cries, and self-torture would
cease as suddenly as they had begun. In either event
there was no aftermath of sullenness, but his return
to normality was complete. Speaking in later years
of these outbursts, he remarked with whimsical humor: "I had a fixed notion that what I wanted I
must have. Somehow, that idea has not entirely
deserted me throughout my life. I have always
known what I wanted, and how to get it. As a child,
I got it by tantrums; in mature years, by hard work."

An old lady is still living who saw a good deal of
the Westinghouse family during their residence in
Central Bridge, and for whom George, at the age of
six, conceived a strong attachment. "I remember
just how he looked then," she said the other day.
"I can see still his earnest little face, with its wrinkle
between the blue eyes as if he were already solving
problems, and the way he would turn it up to mine
when he asked some trifling favor. It is true that
he was a tempestuous child, and would fly now and

then into a fearful passion ; but I suspect that he was not so much to blame for this as were his older brothers and the hired men about the place. They all seemed to take delight in teasing him, to see what he would do.

"He had a strong side, nevertheless, which showed itself even then, and at times when you would least expect it. One day when he had committed some mischief his father called him into an inner room and whipped him with a switch cut from a tree. The switch broke in two or three places, and with a gesture of impatience Mr. Westinghouse threw it aside, exclaiming: 'Pshaw! This is good for nothing.' George, who had been crying lustily, desisted long enough to point to a leather whip which hung from a hook on the wall, and say: 'There's a better one, Father.' His apparent interest in having the thing done properly if it must be done at all proved too much for his father's sobriety, and he was spared further punishment."

CHAPTER II

"The Age 'Twixt Boy and Youth"

Not long after George's birth Mr. and Mrs. Westinghouse, finding themselves somewhat cramped for room in the house where they were living, removed to a larger one a little farther down the point. On the new premises stood a sawmill and a gristmill, the conduct of which devolved upon Mr. Westinghouse, so that he had to hire more workmen. In the new home three boys were born: two, Henry and Herman, died in infancy; the third, Henry Herman, generally known as Herman, was named in memory of them. Increased domestic expenses, together with a business competition which was already making itself felt, led Mr. Westinghouse to consider means of reducing the cost of his machines. Though he could make the wooden parts in his shop and do the assembling there, he had to buy all his metal castings in Schenectady and haul them over by wagon — a tedious and expensive process when the roads were out of repair. When, therefore, his business had sufficiently expanded, he decided to remove both factory and family to Schenectady, and in 1856 the change was made. Two partners named Clute having joined him, the firm bought a building formerly used as a cement mill, on the south bank of the Erie

Canal near the junction of Washington Avenue and the River Road, and turned it into a shop. The main part of this is still standing, though almost hidden by the pretentious structures which have grown up around it; and one can trace from a neighboring elevation what the elements have left of the old sign, "G. Westinghouse & Co.", painted in black letters on the rough limestone surface of the eastern gable end.

During their residence in Schenectady, the family lived in three houses successively. That in which they finally settled down about 1860 is now known as Number 16 State Street. It is a substantial dwelling built of brick with stone and iron trimmings, and has of late years received additions which about double its original capacity. Here the older boys grew to manhood, all developing the individuality to be expected of the sons of so masterful a father. As soon as they reached suitable ages, Mr. Westinghouse took them, one by one, into his shop, for a drill in the rudiments of mechanical work. Jay, the eldest, was also given a course at the Polytechnic Institute in Troy; but on his return it soon became obvious that his most appropriate place was elsewhere than at the bench. He had executive ability and a wise discernment, including a bent for managing men without friction, which would have made their mark in a larger field; and before long he was transferred to a desk in the office, where he met customers, engaged workmen, and kept the accounts. John, next in age, had mechanical gifts of a high order, coupled later in life with a marked religious instinct which led him to devote much of his spare time to what we should now call "social work" among the less favored elements in the community. He was particularly successful in rescuing "gang" boys from a life of crime and starting them on paths toward useful citizenship. In the shop he found metal-working more to his taste than carpentry, so he handled the iron parts of the machines for which the wooden parts were constructed under his father's supervision. Albert, the third son, showed from the outset less taste for mechanics, his chief natural inclinations being toward books. He enjoyed good literature, and argued ingeniously any question which arose in the domestic circle. In the opinion of family friends, he might have had a brilliant career if educated for the bar.

Young George, though he waked up more after the removal to Schenectady, did not expand mentally in the direction his father had hoped. He was sent to school, but took only a languid interest in his studies, though he profited somewhat by his more enlivening companionship. Of this, however, he could not reap the fullest advantage, as his father was able to see little virtue in play, regarding it simply as a form of idleness, and preferring that George should come into the shop every day after school hours and learn how tools were used by skilled hands. But here came again the sense of constraint against which every fiber of the boy's nature had always revolted. To stand at the elbow of a mature man for an hour and watch the plying of saw and plane, the boring of holes, and the driving of screws was a dreary occupation for him. When, for a change, he **was** shifted over to the neighborhood of his brother John, and looked on at the latter's handling of the metal parts, he felt more at liberty to criticize, and before five minutes had elapsed the two lads would be in a heated controversy, in which the temper of each would occasionally break bounds. If, on the other hand, he was taken away from all the rest of the workers and set at a bench by himself, with a pattern before him and the material and tools at hand for making a duplicate of it, his attention would soon wander from his fixed task and he would become immersed in some mechanism of his own contriving — a little engine, or a miniature water wheel with fanciful connections, or what not.

Tinkering in this fashion, sometimes alone and sometimes in company with a schoolmate of similar tastes, he gradually accumulated a collection of incomplete machines, which his conservative father denounced as "trumpery" and would from time to time consign to the scrap heap. Most of the workmen found something amusing in this conflict of wills; but one day when Mr. Westinghouse had broken up and thrown out an apparatus in the construction of which George had displayed uncommon ingenuity, a good-natured foreman whose sympathies had been going out more and more strongly toward the lad stayed after closing time, and, without his employer's knowledge, fitted up a small den in the loft of the building. This he turned over to George for an amateur workshop, and in it the young inventor passed many happy hours, and, near the end of his occupancy, designed and built a model for a rotary engine.

After hanging about the shop for a year or two in an irregular way, George had a serious talk with his father. Mr. Westinghouse had been remonstrating with him for his waste of time, and contrasting his indifference with the earnestness of most of the working force, when George unexpectedly retorted:

"Those men are paid for whatever they do for you. What I do brings me in nothing."

It was the first sign he had ever given of a thrifty spirit, and Mr. Westinghouse improved the opportunity to ask:

"What do you consider your services worth?"

"I don't know; but they must be worth something."

"Well, George, I'll give you a chance to show what you can do. Beginning next Monday, I'll pay you fifty cents for every full day you put in here on something useful. Saturdays, as there is no school, you'll be able to work all day; other afternoons, you can charge up your work by the hour till you have made a whole day. How will that suit you?"

"I'm ready to try it."

The bargain was struck on the spot, and recorded at the cashier's desk. But George was not yet fourteen years old, and had not lost his liking for a play-spell now and then; so one Saturday when several of his mates were going off for a frolic and urged him to accompany them, he went to his father to serve notice that he should not be at his post that afternoon.   Mr. Westinghouse recognized this as a proper occasion for impressing a lesson.

"A good citizen who makes an agreement to put in his time working," said he solemnly, "doesn't shirk it at the first temptation.   I had a job laid out, that I expected you to start today."

He led the way to a pile of pipe which he wished cut, and gave his son full instructions how to cut it.

"This is hard work and will take you some time," he added — "perhaps all your spare hours for the first half of next week.   I'm going out of town for a few days, and when I come back I hope to find the job about finished."

George uttered no protest.   While his father had been talking his own mind had leaped to a plan, and before noon he had rigged up a combination of tools which, attached to a power machine, would feed the pipe and do the cutting automatically.   Then, after a few words of explanation to the friendly foreman, who promised to keep an eye on things in his absence, he threw off his overalls and joined his comrades for their outing.   When he came home he ran over to the shop and found all the pipe cut as directed.   Until his father returned, therefore, he was free to do what he pleased.

While naturally gratified at this exhibition of the inventive faculty, Mr. Westinghouse became almost hopeless of converting so volatile a boy into a steady mechanic.   One day he mentioned the matter to a neighbor, a clergyman, who suggested that perhaps the lad might do better at something which would call into play his unusually lively imagination.

"I've tried him at all sorts of things," answered Mr. Westinghouse, with a shade of disappointment in his tone, "but his one desire seems to be to avoid work; and you know as well as I do that no young man will ever amount to anything who won't work."

"It would take a good deal to convince me," said the other, "that the laziest boy in the world couldn't be interested in something, if you gave him a wide enough range of choice."

"You'd like to make a preacher of him, perhaps?"

The minister ignored the seeming irony of the suggestion.

"No, I shouldn't try to 'make' him that or anything else. If I have measured him correctly he isn't the kind of boy you can shape against his will. I think you will save time if you let him do his own shaping, and confine yourself to encouraging him when he finds out what he is best fitted to do."

He was moving away, but Mr. Westinghouse detained him by laying a hand on his shoulder.

"Look here, Dominie, all I want is to do what is right, and not to make a mistake which we'll feel sorry for later. Now, you've started me thinking. Tell me what you'd do if the boy were yours."

"Well, I suppose I should not press him into spending all his leisure time in the shop. Let him get out and play more. That will free his mind, and by and by he'll lay hold of an idea that fascinates him, and he'll follow it till it lands him somewhere; he merely hasn't yet found his place in the world. Shall you send him to college?"

"He can go if he cares to."

"That's right.   I'd even advise him, if I were you, to take a course.   College is sometimes a great eye opener."

From that day forward George was allowed a little more time to spend as he chose.   To his father's surprise, he did not waste it absolutely in doing nothing, though he fell into what was, in the elder's eyes, the next worst thing — a habit of tinkering for hours together on some toy device.   His most ambitious amusement, perhaps, was playing with a little boat which he launched on the canal, equipped with a screw propeller engine built almost wholly by his own hands.   Though it was never evident to his father or brothers just what he was trying to do with this craft, there appeared to be lurking in his own mind some conception of a more efficient motor than that which had served him as a model.   Now and then his evolutions with his boat would result in its tipping over, but he never suffered any damage more severe than a soaking, for he had learned to take care of himself pretty well in the water.   And thereby hangs a tale which we may as well recall in passing.

One of the young men in the Westinghouse works was William Ratcliffe, with whom for some time George worked at the same bench.   They grew to be fast friends, and used to put in their infrequent holidays at some job of their own concocting.   Mr. Ratcliffe still owns a sleigh which they built thus in partnership, and which is as good today as on the day they put it together.   They also took a fancy at one time · to make violins.   George had studied the mechanism of one, and believed that he could not only construct an instrument but learn to play it if he could find the right teacher. A few practical efforts in that line, however, convinced him that he had no ear, and he gave up the notion.

Ratcliffe was fond of swimming and soon taught George the art; and in the warm weather the pair used to frequent a spot in the Mohawk which was a favorite with the town boys, who varied their frolics in the water with a few on land, like tying one another's clothes into hard knots, or spiriting them away and leaving the owners to prowl around for a half-hour unclad. To guard against such tricks, the more prudent of the bathers fell into the way of hiding their garments in remote places. George became so enthusiastic about swimming and diving that during the season his mind was full of these sports whenever not immediately occupied with the work he had in hand. One night his parents were awakened by a sound as of some heavy body falling in an adjoining chamber. Running in there, they found George squirming about on the floor stark naked. Their questions at first evoked only a stupid attempt at response; but, as his mind gradually cleared, he explained that he had been dreaming of being on the river bank, and, divesting himself of his scant raiment, he had dived from his bed into what he imagined was deep water, and by a narrow chance had escaped without broken bones. Then came a search for his nightgown, which, under the spell of his dream, he had taken pains to hide from his prankish playmates. All over the upper story of the house prowled father, mother, and son, peering into every nook and cranny which seemed likely to have attracted him, but in vain: and it was not till several days afterward that the missing garment was accidentally discovered, squeezed behind a trunk which stood flat against the wall.

The school George attended was in a building at the corner of Union and College streets, which, having passed through a half-century of vicissitudes, had little about it to gratify the eye or stimulate the ambition of the young people under its roof. To his father's suggestion that he prepare for college, George had assented less because it appealed to him than because he had no particular argument to raise against it. A few of his schoolfellows of this period are still living in Schenectady, and remember George as a rather inept pupil. It was not that his mind was dull; but the books he was required to study failed as a rule to stir his imagination, and he had only an indifferent gift of self-expression. However good an understanding he might have of a subject, as soon as he was called to his feet before his class, his power of translating thought into words seemed to suffer a temporary paralysis, and he would stumble through the exercise as if he were trusting wholly to guesswork. Penmanship and spelling gave him a deal of trouble, and he found grammar a deadly burden. This puzzled most of his teachers, because his logical faculties, when applied to something which had captured his fancy, struck them as considerably above the average. He was also keen as to everything mathematical, and in free-hand drawing he excelled all competitors with circles that were round, and lines that were straight, and angles that measured the required number of degrees.

Only one member of the school faculty appears to have fully comprehended him. This was a woman who combined unusual skill as an instructor with a most attractive personality and a sympathetic manner. George surrendered himself unreservedly to her gentle sway. She seemed to recognize in him a certain quality not found in the other boys she taught, and to have an intuitive sense of the reasons why he hated one thing and liked another with such intensity; and she adapted her treatment of him to these peculiarities. As a result, he was almost romantic in his attachment to her, and the impress she made on his life was always gratefully acknowledged by him, his appreciation manifesting itself in many kindnesses he was able to extend to her in later years.

In the midst of his preparatory schooling came on the Civil War, and George, though only fourteen years of age, was smitten with the prevalent martial fever. So were two of his brothers, Albert and John. Mr. Westinghouse was an ardent patriot, but he knew little of the spirit with which the Southern States had entered the Confederacy, and believed, like so many other loyalists in the North, that the hostilities would not last long after the Government had made a real show of strength. Hence, when the older boys expressed their purpose to enlist, he advised them to wait a while, and they reluctantly consented. John persisted, however, in hovering about the recruiting officers who came that way, and used to regale George, as they worked together on Saturdays, with a rehearsal of the war stories gleaned from these men. George had gradually developed a preference for working in metals over working in wood; John had encouraged this tendency, and they had formed a habit of coöperating in various small-scale engineering enterprises. Their talks about soldiering had stimulated George to a degree where he was ready to do something desperate for the sake of getting a taste of the real experience. In his own mind he reasoned out the situation about like this: Albert and John both wished to go to war but were prevented because they had been so imprudent as to mention the subject in the family circle; his wise plan, therefore, would be to avoid interference by holding his tongue till the psychological moment, and then running away.

He was tall for his age, and uncommonly mature of countenance; and though his figure was spare, his large bones and good muscles indicated that he would in due time acquire a sturdy build. Unfortunately for his project, he was by nature too candid to be a successful secret-keeper; and this trait, as well as a boyish craving for companionship, led him to take half a dozen of his best friends into his confidence and propose that they all run away together and not return till they had distinguished themselves by deeds of valor on the battlefield. The suggestion was not generally received with warmth; many of the boys agreed that it would be a great lark, but did not dare invite the parental wrath by so bold a defiance; others thought they might try it later, after they saw how their home-folk took the news of some other fellow's escapade. When the time for a final decision arrived, only one comrade was ready to go with him the whole length, and at once.

One morning Mrs. Westinghouse had occasion to call upon George to do an errand for her, but was unable to find him anywhere about the house. She felt sure that he had not gone to school, for his strapful of books still lay where he had tossed it the afternoon before. Having looked for him upstairs and down, and called his name repeatedly from front windows and back, she gave up the search. A neighbor came in breathless, with the information that George had been seen that morning walking toward the railroad station with a carpetbag in his hand, and apparently trying to avoid observation.

"Are you positive it was *my* George?" demanded the mother, too astonished to trust her hearing.

"There is no question about it," the visitor assured her; "and one of the boys next door says George has been telling him for some time that he was watching his chance to run away and go to war."

In another minute Mrs. Westinghouse had dispatched her housemaid to the Works with a message to her husband, apprising him of these unexpected developments. The good man did not seem at all upset, but, with a quick glance at the clock, reached for his hat and quitted the building.

George, meanwhile, having put into a carpetbag a few essential articles of clothing, had slipped away soon after breakfast and taken his course through back streets and alleys to the station, where an accommodation train was made up daily for the East. He found his co-conspirator already on hand, though not quite so enthusiastic as at their latest previous meeting, and, as they had a few minutes to wait, George improved the time by pumping fresh vigor into the other boy's resolution; then, the train having drawn up on the track in front of them, they were able to enter the nearest car and settle down in a forward seat headed for their hearts' desire. The minutes lagged like hours while the adult passengers climbed on one by one, and George had considerable difficulty in keeping his back turned toward the rear of the car in such a way as to elude recognition by any of his parents' friends who might be traveling that morning.

At last the fateful instant came. The conductor sounded his brisk warning outside, "All aboard!", entered the car in which the boys sat, and promptly reached for the bell rope. Before he had a chance to pull it, however, appeared another actor on the scene. He was a man about fifty years of age, of stalwart frame, clad in a gray cloth suit and a soft hat, and wearing an expression on his face which was certainly serious and perhaps a trifle stern. Boarding the train as if he owned it, he called to the conductor to wait a moment. Everybody in the car turned to see who thus peremptorily held it back — everybody, that is, except George: he did not need to turn, for he had recognized the voice, and a sudden chill had run down his spine as he heard it. He was conscious that the newcomer was taking long strides through the car from rear to front; then he glanced up to see his father standing before him, with a beckoning finger outstretched. Mr. Westinghouse was not at all excited in manner, or apparently out of breath, though he had been obliged to hurry more than was his wont. He uttered no reproaches, he did not even raise his voice above its ordinary pitch as he said: "George, I guess you'd better come back home!"

As was customary with any one to whom Mr. Westinghouse began a suggestion with his characteristic "I guess you'd better," no time was wasted about complying. There was no debate, no questioning, no explanation or other dilatory recourse. George, thoroughly crestfallen, fished out his carpet-bag from under the seat and followed his father to the rear door and down the platform steps, looking to neither right nor left. He was dimly aware that his martial-minded companion was treading closely on his heels, and that the feet of the trio were barely firm on the ground before the belated bell rang, the whistle responded, and the train which was to have borne him to glory was off without him.

Mr. Westinghouse walked home with his son and saw him start for school, where a tardy mark was waiting for him; this he did not mind very much, but there was also a sardonic grin on the faces of some of the mates to whom he had confided his plans, and this he did mind a good deal. However, his feelings were considerably salved when he met his family at the noonday meal and observed their general disposition to ignore the incident till, just before they were leaving the table, his father said: "Perhaps,

George, when you are old enough to know your own mind and understand what it all means — if the war lasts 'till then — you may be free to go.   But don't count on it too surely.   I hope there'll be an end to the fighting long before that."

CHAPTER III

SOLDIER AND SAILOR, STUDENT AND SWAIN

BY the summer of 1862, Mr. Westinghouse had changed his mind about the duration of the war, and in August Albert enlisted in the Sixth New York Volunteer Cavalry. During the ill-fated advance toward Richmond in the spring of 1863 he was taken prisoner at Spottsylvania Court House, but was paroled a few days later, and in September was transferred to the Second New York Veteran Volunteer Cavalry, with a lieutenant's commission. Meanwhile conscription had begun, a drawing was announced to be held in Schenectady, and John was able to face his father with the fact that the only alternative now lay between offering his services to the Government voluntarily and taking his chance of having to render them under compulsion. Mr. Westinghouse admitted that this was true, and withdrew all further objection to his volunteering. He therefore took immediate advantage of an offer, made him some time before, of an appointment as an Acting Third Assistant Engineer in the navy, and set off for Washington to see about it.

George, spurred to fresh activity by John's example, reopened the subject with his father by a reminder that he was now nearly seventeen, sound and strong, and presumably as well able as he would be later to judge for himself in such matters.

"Perhaps you are right, my son," assented Mr. Westinghouse, and that afternoon George packed his effects for the next move.

As John had procured his commission through his father's partners, one of whom possessed considerable influence with their Representative in Congress, George went to them to find out whether they could not get for him also an appointment to a position where he would have machinery to handle, and an assignment to the same ship on which John was serving. When they told him that that was out of the question, he decided to try for the army instead, in the hope that by some good luck he might find his way to where his brother Albert was. Accordingly, he sought a recruiting station in New York, where he laid his desires before the officer in charge.

"I'm afraid," remarked that gentleman, eyeing him critically, and with a half-repressed smile which George could not then understand, "we can't do all you wish right away. Just now it looks as if Lee's army may break through into Pennsylvania, and we are busy enlisting an emergency force to drive him back if he attempts it. You've never served before, you say?"

"No," said George, "I'm only seventeen, and my father's kept me back till now."

The officer's face sobered again, and his voice was very kindly as he replied:

"I see — I see. Well, how would you like to try

GEORGE WESTINGHOUSE
From a War Time Portrait

the thirty-days' service for a start? It will give you a little experience, and show you how well soldiering agrees with you. We're trying to fill up the Twelfth. Will you sign?"

"What position can I get in the regiment, if I do?"

"I fancy you will have to take a gun and a knapsack, my boy, until you've proved what's in you. Once in the field, it will depend on yourself how far up you climb."

"All right. That suits me."

George signed the roll and dropped into his place at the tail of a squad who were about to be looked over by the surgeon. Two days later he was off for the front.

At the end of his brief experimental term, which was marked by no exciting episode, he was more desirous than ever of seeing some real soldier life; so he offered himself as a three-years' recruit for the Sixteenth New York Volunteer Cavalry. Here he renewed his inquiry about a commission.

"You are rather young to shoulder the responsibilities of an officer," was the answer.

"But I've already been broken in," he pleaded, "and I've learned a thing or two about taking care of men."

"Why don't your raise a company of your own, then, and command it?"

"I would in a minute, if I had the chance."

"That can be managed, I dare say, as far as the chance is concerned. Where would you go for your men?"

"Back in Schoharie County, where I was born.

I know lots of fellows out there who'd enlist if we only got hold of them the right way."

To his surprise and pleasure, George received the next morning an assignment to recruiting duty in the district he had named, coupled with the condition that, if he brought back fifty acceptable men, he would be recommended for a lieutenancy. He went off in high spirits, visiting first his old home, Central Bridge, which he found pretty well stripped of available material, though two men promised to join his troop. At Schoharie, Middleburg, and other well-settled points in the county, he discovered a like state of affairs. Then he pushed for the outlying country. A favorite resort of his boyhood had been the picturesque neighborhood of Fultonham, where Lorenzo Stewart, an old and valued employee of his father's, was living. Stewart took a lively interest in George's errand, but held out few hopes of success.

"I suspect this part of the county is short of the kind of young men you are after," he explained, going over the names, one by one, of the farmer boys they both knew. Most of the eligibles, it appeared, had already gone south with the 134th New York.

"All right," said George, "then I'll try my luck with the slouters."

"Slouters" was the cant term used locally to designate a thriftless class of people who lived back among the hills, subsisting ordinarily nobody knew how, and descending into the valleys only when cold or hunger forced them to seek a short job of work.

"It will do you no good to go there, either," Stewart assured him. "John Cater has got ahead of you. He came back from the army, all dressed up and sleek-looking, and carried off every slouter in sight."

But George was out for game, and would not let himself be diverted from his quest. Stewart stood by him manfully, and took pains to see that he should be included in all the "apple cuts" and other rustic merrymakings held thereabout during his stay. The fine-looking young soldier in his smart uniform created no slight flutter among the assembled maidens, and put their swains to the blush for some excuse for not themselves wearing the blue. George thoroughly enjoyed his visit among the scenes of his childhood, now that he had become a person of more consequence. It was a sore disappointment, however, that he could pick up only his two recruits at Central Bridge and fifteen elsewhere in the county; but with this small contingent he reported at head-quarters, nursing the hope that a commission might be issued to him in view of all he had tried to do.

"Too bad, my boy, but you can't turn seventeen into fifty," was the good-humored but positive response to all his arguments. Back to the war, therefore, went George again as a private soldier. Of what he did and how he fared in his second term of service, not much is known, beyond the fact that the experience was in some respects disappointing. He had joined the cavalry expecting that it would be easier to ride than to walk, but was disillusioned by the discovery that he would have to take care of his horse every night before getting any rest for himself. His campaigning was confined to northern Virginia;

it consisted chiefly of scouting duty, designed to out-
wit the tricks of Mosby's guerrillas and involving a
maximum of hard work for a minimum of glory.

Although in later years he enjoyed his participation
in the war as a reminiscence, he never volunteered it
as a topic of conversation.   When some other veteran
of the citizen soldiery was dining with him they would
exchange recollections, or when some of his more
youthful guests would question him he would talk
most pleasantly about his army life, telling how he
and his camp mates soaked their hard-tack in frying-
pan grease to make it eatable, and cooked bacon and
chicken in the open fire wrapped in paper and
smothered in clay; how they captured a pig against
orders; how he once made a bread pudding with his
own hands and how good it tasted; what happened
to him on picket duty, and the like.   To all who
heard him tell these stories, it was a subject of regret
that during his military service he kept no diary or
other personal memoranda.   He was not fond of
composition, and only a few fragments of his sparse
correspondence are still preserved.

From a letter sent home in December by a Schenectady boy in the Second New York Veteran Cavalry, we learn that George had recently been at Camp
Stoneman, near Washington, to visit his brother
Albert, then a lieutenant with a splendid record for
gallantry and efficiency.   From the same note it
appears that a man-of-war had just arrived at the
Washington Navy Yard with John Westinghouse
aboard, and that the brothers were to have a reunion.
Odds and ends of information, gathered from various

sources and pieced together, indicate that all three boys were furloughed to spend Christmas with their friends in the North. A family gathering was to be held at the house of a relative in New York, and the brothers, with a young cousin, were on the way to it when, as they passed the barracks in City Hall Park, Albert left his companions to enter the building for a brief errand. He rejoined them in a few minutes with an air of deep concern.

"I can't go with you, after all," he said. "I must return to camp at once." With that he shook hands all round in farewell and reëntered the barracks. Their glimpse of his receding figure as the door closed behind him was the last any of the party ever saw of him. A little later he and his men sailed for New Orleans.

On Christmas day, 1864, just one year after the marred festivity, it fell to Herman, then a lad of eleven, to break to his parents the news of Albert's death in the battle of McLeod's Mills, Louisiana. He received it from a neighbor who had lost a son in the same fight. Mr. Westinghouse bore the blow with the stoic resignation of a man who had long ago counted the cost; Mrs. Westinghouse was terribly broken by it, and was never the same woman afterward. Albert had been distinctly the " mother's boy " of the little group.

A few months before this, George, who still had a yearning to try his hand at marine engineering, had decided to shift from the army to the navy. Soon after joining the cavalry he had risen to be a corporal, but promotion beyond that threatened to be slow;

and on December 1, 1864, by virtue of his good military record, and of an examination which, thanks to his mechanical training, he passed with marked credit, he was appointed an Acting Third Assistant Engineer and ordered at once to duty on the ship *Muscoota*. Later he served on the *Stars and Stripes*, and in the Potomac flotilla. His friend Ratcliffe, loyal to their youthful companionship, lent him a lathe to keep on shipboard, and with its aid he improved his odd hours in building a small model of a sawbuck engine.

The next year the war ended. George came home in the summer, and John, who meanwhile had been promoted one grade, followed late in the autumn. George showed a marked improvement as the result of his experience in the armed service. Before leaving home he had been considerably developed on his social side and learned to control his temper, through his association with so many boys of his own age at the high school. To this his discipline as soldier and sailor had added the habit of standing straighter and bearing himself with dignity, and of applying a keener observation to everything. He never seemed to be seeking for new ideas, but absorbed them wherever he went, and after they had been duly digested they always bore fruit in experiment. His father was pleased with his increased manliness and quickened senses, but did not understand his mental processes much better than of old; to all his family, indeed, he still seemed a good deal of a dreamer.

It was doubtless this conception which prompted his father to remind him, within a few days of his return, of his agreement to take a college course. He did not need the reminder, having already begun preparation for his academic martyrdom by taking some of his old school textbooks from the shelf on which they had lain untouched during his absence, and running over a few subjects on which he felt uncertain. The records of Union College show that he was admitted to the scientific department, sophomore class, on the fifteenth of September, 1865. The college then contained one hundred and ninety students, all of whom, according to the published rules, were expected to live on the campus, though in George's case this requirement was relaxed at his father's solicitation so that he could live at home.

Of the personality of George at this period we glean a hint here and there which shows that it must have impressed the minds of his mates rather deeply in order to have enabled them to remember it as well as some of them do after the lapse of a half century. The Reverend Walter Scott of Boston, for example, pictures him as a tall, well-proportioned young man, with an air of self-reliance and an unusually mature appearance. "I recall," says Mr. Scott, "his energetic walk across the campus to the engineering rooms. He had the manner of a man with a definite purpose, pursuing a straight course toward that end. I think he mingled little with the students, owing probably to his absorption in mechanical studies and also to the fact that he had no room in the college buildings."

Other contemporaries bear like witness, though none whom I have been able to reach has gone much into detail as to George's mode of life before and after his working hours, his associations, or his

nontechnical tastes. One reason for this perhaps
lies in the shortness of his collegiate career, for
he left about the Christmas holidays. His class
register gives him a mark of 12.50 for the fall term,
the highest mark won by any one for the year being
25.50. These figures are not especially enlightening,
as the scale on which they were based cannot now be
ascertained; but the weight of evidence indicates
that he did not distinguish himself in the sphere of
book-learning. He was repeatedly absent with no
better excuse than his desire to look on at some mechanical operation then in progress in the town or
neighborhood, appearing quite oblivious of the fact
that college classes could not be conducted on a basis
of haphazard attendance.

The lines of study pursued during the fall term
were the French and German languages, solid geometry, and English rhetoric, essays, and vocal training. In the geometry sessions he seems to have had
no difficulty in keeping his attention fixed, but the
English branches were tiresome to him. For the
foreign tongues he had neither taste nor talent, and
made no secret of the fact. Professor William Wells,
who taught them, used to declare as the fruit of a
long experience that it was folly to attempt to proph-
esy the man from the boy, citing the case of young
Westinghouse as his most potent illustration. "He
was my despair," Doctor Wells would explain. "Not
only was it impossible to stir his active interest in the
work of the class, but, while the other boys were
struggling with German syntax or French pronuncia-
tion, he would amuse himself making pencil drawings

on his wristbands. His sketches were always of locomotives, stationary engines, or something of that sort."

In view of the way he had spent so much of his time, George was not greatly surprised at receiving a message one day from Doctor Hickok, the acting head of the college, asking him to call at the president's office, and he responded in expectation of a severe scolding if nothing worse. It did surprise him to have the Doctor greet him in the pleasantest manner, invite him to be seated, and open their conversation with the inquiry:

"Westinghouse, how do you like college, now that you have given it a little trial?"

For a moment George was at a loss for an answer; he could not honestly say that he liked it, though on the other hand he was fair-minded enough to realize that this was less the fault of the college than his own.

"I dare say I should like it very well," he said, after a short pause, "if I had time to give my mind to my studies." He then proceeded to explain at length certain inventions he was engaged in trying to develop.

It was now Doctor Hickok's turn to be taken at a disadvantage; he had not looked for such frankness, or for so lucid an exposition of the mechanical principles involved in George's plans.

"After what you have told me," said he, "it is plain that you would be wasting your time and your gifts in staying here and pursuing studies in which you have no heart. I will see your father at once, and put your case before him."

George drew a deep sigh of relief. If so high an authority as Doctor Hickok advised his following his natural bent, he felt sure of being released from his compact and allowed to return to the occupations he loved. This assumption proved correct, though Mr. Westinghouse shook his head sadly over the collapse of his hope of making George a scholar — a hope born of his fancied discovery that his son would never be good for much of anything else! But, pitiful as the admission of failure might be, he granted it with the best grace he could, and told George he might go to work at the bench. George hesitated.

"Well, what's the matter?" asked Mr. Westinghouse.

"We might as well settle the wage now, Father."

"You can have the same pay you were getting when you left off — a dollar a day, wasn't it?"

"Nine shillings. That was enough for the boy I was before I went away; but I am practically a man now, and if I am worth anything I am worth a man's wages. Give me two dollars a day and I stay here; otherwise I go where I can get that."

"I had intended, George, to start you again at the old figure and give you an opportunity to show how much more you were worth to the business. If you had done well, you would have earned promotion soon. However, I am willing to give you a trial at two dollars, on the understanding that if you fall short of what is expected of you we go back to nine shillings."

Apparently George laid himself out to prove his

value to his father, lending a hand wherever he could be useful. Regardless of what he might be doing, however, his mind was busy with one special topic, of which the suggestion had grown out of his service in the navy. Before he left home he had built a rotary engine, which was novel enough in some of its features to secure a patent. His life on shipboard, though short, had enabled him to study marine engineering on its practical side, and all his investigations had tended to confirm his original belief that in this field, if not everywhere, the rotary principle was bound to supersede the reciprocating in the construction of motive machinery. Now and then his restlessness would get the better of him, and he would grasp at the chance of going away from Schenectady to transact an outside negotiation for the firm.

It was while returning from one such expedition to Albany that he was held up by an accident of not infrequent occurrence in those days of small rails and light rolling stock. Two rear cars of a train running just ahead of his had jumped the track, and all traffic on that section was blocked for two hours. George and a fellow traveler spent most of the time watching the wrecking crew as they grappled with one car after another, painfully prying it back, inch by inch, till it could be finally jacked over to its place on the track. As the work neared its end, George, who had been unusually silent for several minutes, remarked with some impatience: "That was a poorly handled job!"

"It was tedious," admitted his friend, "but that couldn't be helped."

"Yes, it could. They could have done the whole thing in fifteen minutes by clamping a pair of rails to the track, and running them off at an angle like a frog, so as to come up even against the wheels of the nearest derailed car. Then, by hitching an engine to the car, they could have shunted it back into place. In fact, it wouldn't be a bad idea for a railroad company to put together a car-replacer on that principle, and have it on hand for use in emergencies."

"Why don't you make one and sell it to the railroads?"

"That's a good idea. I'll do it."

Before he went to bed that night George had thought out his plan. The next morning he made his drawings, and as soon as he had prepared a model he carried it to his father. Mr. Westinghouse examined it, but without expressing great enthusiasm.

"It will cost money to carry out that scheme," he said as he handed back the model. "If it's worth anything, somebody will steal your idea — "

"I shall patent it, of course," George broke in.

"Yes, yes, I know. But you will have to pay the Government's charges and your lawyer's fees, and then will come the expense of manufacturing and marketing. You'll let yourself in for a pretty penny before you're through; and where's the money coming from?"

"I thought probably you'd lend it to me."

"My son, if I have learned one lesson in life, it is, to stick to things I know something about. Now, I do know threshing machines, and horse powers, and all that, but I don't know railroads. Neither do you. If you are bound to go into this business, I don't suppose I can stop you; but you will have to make my share a very small one."

George realized that when his father took such a stand it was time thrown away to argue the question. But his belief that he had a good idea had not been weakened by the discussion, and, with his father's little contribution in his pocket, he seized his first opportunity to call upon several men in the city who were recognized as shrewd investors and laid his plan before them. Some put him aside with slight attention, but two of his business acquaintances were willing to risk small sums in his venture. A partnership was thus formed, each of the two capitalists contributing five thousand dollars and George his father's modicum of money and the right to use his patent. Under their contract, also, he was to travel for the concern.

The work done on this device had brought him into contact with other problems of railway construction and operation, among them being the making of a more durable frog than the cast-iron ones then in use. This part of a railroad track is subjected to severe service, and the wear upon it is so great that frequent replacing of the frogs was necessary, involving a heavy cost for material and labor and serious interference with traffic during replacement. The remedy Westinghouse proposed was the employment of cast steel instead of cast iron and the making of the frog reversible, so that when one side was worn out it could be turned over. By the combined use of the more durable metal and the feature of reversal, the life of the frog was increased more than twentyfold, resulting in its very extended employment. The right to use his patent on this invention he assigned to the firm, as he had his replacer patent.

In connection with this development, it is interesting to record the fact that Westinghouse was probably the first man, in our country at least, and possibly in the world, to produce steel castings, as that term is now applied. This is an art that has very slowly developed through many difficulties until it has attained a most important status in metallurgical production. He knew nothing about the subject except what he had picked up by scant opportunities for observation in early attempts to have his car-replacers and frogs made at existing steel plants; but he saw no reason why steel castings could not be produced, and so went ahead with his plans to the extent that was necessary for his particular purpose.

The experimental car-replacers and frogs were made at Troy, New York, and at Pompton, New Jersey. It was after he had invented the frog, but before his patent on it had been issued, that, having been to Pompton to ascertain what arrangements he could make for its manufacture, he was starting for home from New York by the Hudson River Railroad, when he met with an adventure which gave a fresh zest to his life. His train was crowded with passengers. He could have found a seat in the smoking car, but as he did not smoke he preferred trying his fortune elsewhere. Not until he reached the last car did he find a vacant place, and that was beside a young woman whose appearance attracted him instantly. In a few minutes he had engaged her in conversation and drawn forth the information that her home was in Roxbury, New York, but that she had friends in Brooklyn, and was now on her way to visit relatives in Kingston. Shortly before she reached her destination, he expressed the hope that she would allow him to continue their acquaintance. The modest hesitancy with which she received the suggestion reminded him that she knew nothing about him except what he had incidentally let fall in the course of their chat; and, with characteristic resourcefulness, he tore a page from his notebook and scribbled on it the addresses of three or four substantial persons who could answer any questions concerning his antecedents and character. She appeared to be reassured by his manner, for she consented to his calling upon her, and when he remounted the car platform after helping her off he was as jubilant as if he had won a great triumph. The first thing he did on reaching Schenectady was to seek the pastor of the church he attended, and ask him to write a letter to the young lady, stating who he was, and the standing of the Westinghouses in the community.

His family was struck with his light-heartedness when he came to the tea table that evening, and one of his sisters rallied him a little on it.

"You look as if you had won a prize in a lottery," she said.

"I am not sure that I have won it yet," he responded, "but I think I have a good chance."

Mr. and Mrs. Westinghouse exchanged quick glances. Both disapproved strongly of anything in the nature of gambling, and were somewhat startled at his confession. He let the whole party puzzle over his case for a few minutes before he explained:

"I've met the woman I am going to marry."

Mr. Westinghouse regarded him with a quizzical air.

"The woman you are going to marry, eh?" he commented, with mock seriousness "And are you proposing to support her, or is she to support you?"

"I've no fear that I can't take care of a wife," was George's self-sufficient answer.

"You haven't built your house yet, I suppose?"

"No, we may come here for a while and build the house later."

"Ah!"

That was all anybody said at the time, but that George was in earnest was evident when, after two visits to Kingston and three to Roxbury, he announced to his mother that he was the accepted lover of Marguerite Erskine Walker; that they had decided to be married in Brooklyn on the eighth of the following August, and that he would like to bring his wife home till they could find a house suited to their needs and purse.

GEORGE WESTINGHOUSE AND MRS. WESTINGHOUSE
DURING THEIR EARLIER DAYS OF WEDDED LIFE

CHAPTER IV

Opportunity Knocks at the Door

To the reader whose traveling days have fallen within the last quarter-century, the air brake in use on the modern railroad is so much a matter of course that it might have existed from the beginning of time. How recent an invention it is, and what a revolution it has accomplished, can be appreciated only by those of us who can remember the conditions that prevailed before its coming.

Hand-braking was both difficult and dangerous. A brakeman stood between every two cars on a passenger train, and, at a point about half a mile from the next stopping place, he would begin to turn a horizontal handwheel on one platform so as to tighten slowly a chain that set the brakes on a single pair of wheels. When he had wound the chain taut he would step across to the opposite platform and repeat the operation on the handwheel there. No matter how skilled all the brakemen on a train might be, their work was always uneven, for no two cars would respond to the brake with the same promptness, and the slower ones would bump into the quicker, adding to the hazards of the task. A freight train was harder to care for than a passenger train, because the brakemen had to ride on top of the cars in all weathers, with the liability of being knocked off by a low bridge, frozen in midwinter, or, on windy or slippery nights, missing their footing and falling between the cars.

These possibilities and others were brought vividly before the mind of young Westinghouse one day when he was on his way from Schenectady to Troy to meet an engagement at the Bessemer Steel Works. His train coming to a sudden standstill midway between stations, he got off, with several fellow passengers, to ascertain the cause of the delay. A short distance ahead the distorted hulks of two locomotives, and a stretch of track strewn with overturned or broken cars and the remains of what had been a solid cargo of merchandise, told their story: two heavily loaded freight trains had come together with a crash. The day was clear, the roadbed at that point was level, the track was well railed and smooth and straight; it seemed as if a collision could hardly have occurred except through gross carelessness. Westinghouse suggested as much to one of the company's employees who was standing near, supervising the clearing of the track.

"No," answered the man, "the engineers saw each other, and both tried their best to stop, but they couldn't."

"Why not? Wouldn't the brakes work?"

"Oh, yes, but there wasn't time. You can't stop a train in a moment."

This remark rang in the young man's ears the rest of the day. Fortunately, no lives had been lost in the wreck, but his train was delayed so long that he missed his appointment, and the annoyance gave pungency to questions which kept rising in his mind : They hadn't time? Why not? Suppose one of those trains had been full of passengers instead of freight? Suppose it had been the train he was riding on? Here was a subject even better worth studying than the replacement of derailed cars, which had commanded so much of his attention as the result of an earlier accident.

Obviously, the key to the collision lay in the lapse of time between the "down brakes" whistle and the clamping of the brake shoes on the wheels. The engineers doubtless acted quickly enough when they apprehended the danger; but, if, instead of sounding a signal to several other men, these two had been able to apply the brakes instantly themselves, the possibilities of damage would at least have been reduced to a minimum. How could this be made practicable?

The first idea that occurred to him was to connect the brakes on the several cars with the coupling mechanism in such a way that when the steam was shut off and the brakes were set on the locomotive by the engineer, the consequent closing-up of the cars would automatically set their brakes also. A few experiments, however, with a miniature apparatus rigged up in his father's shop, convinced him that the scheme would be quite unworkable if the ounces of his little model were translated into the tons of a real train. Walking one Sunday afternoon past a siding on which stood a few idle freight cars, another thought came to him : Why would it not be perfectly feasible to extend underneath the whole train a long brake chain, which could be suddenly drawn taut by some device close to the hand of the engineer, and thus bring all the brakes into action? While he was still pondering this question, business called him to Chicago. Here he was talking one day with Superintendent Towne of the Chicago, Burlington and Quincy Railroad, when the conversation turned upon increasing the safety of trains by better braking facilities.

"Come in tomorrow afternoon," he said to Westinghouse, as they parted, "and we'll go down to the yard where they make up our prize train, the Aurora Accommodation. We've put a brake on that which seems to do all that can be done in the brake line. I'll have the inventor over to meet you, and we'll inspect the train together. You'll find him an interesting fellow, and he'll talk brake with you from morning till night if you'll let him."

Westinghouse gladly accepted the invitation. He found the inventor sociability itself, but when he let drop a remark that he, too, was thinking over a braking contrivance, it was not very hospitably received.

"You are throwing away your time, young man," the inventor presently asserted, with an air of finality. "I went all over the ground before completing my invention, and my patents are broad enough to cover everything."

But Westinghouse was not to be so easily frightened off. The brake, as he noted on examination, consisted of a windlass on the locomotive, which could be revolved by pressing a grooved wheel against the flange of the driving wheel, so as to wind up a chain that ran underneath the entire train, just as he had tentatively figured. That the two men should have hit upon the same fundamental feature was not strange, if we reflect that up to that hour no road in the United States used a brake which was not moved by a chain.

The chain of the apparatus was carried along its course by running over a series of rollers connected with the brake levers of every car in such a manner that, as soon as the chain was tightened, the brakes came instantly against the wheels. To Westinghouse the windlass arrangement seemed clumsy, incapable of accurate control, and subject to rapid deterioration under wear. For this, he believed a steam cylinder might be substituted, placed beneath and supplied with steam from the engine, its piston being so connected as to draw the chain taut when desired. Then arose a troublesome question. The Burlington train which was undergoing demonstration consisted of only four or five cars, whereas what he was aiming to devise was a cab-controlled brake system for a train made up of two or three times as many cars and requiring a chain of correspondingly greater length; and where was the locomotive which could carry a cylinder capable of taking up so much slack?

To meet this difficulty, he conceived the idea of supplying all the cars with separate cylinders, fed from the engine by connections between the cars. But here came in the factor of temperature; for even in warm weather the steam would be condensed before it had reached the hindmost car, while in winter the condensed steam would freeze. Plainly, he would have to seek some other agency than steam for transmitting power from the cab.

"Opportunity," says the familiar maxim, "knocks once at every man's door." The guise in which it knocked at George Westinghouse's door is worthy of a place among the romances of invention.

It was the noon hour in the office of the Westinghouse Works on the canal bank. The heads of the concern had gone home for dinner, and the underlings who had brought their lunches with them were gathered in groups, talking. Apart from the rest sat George Westinghouse at a table, but looking out of the window as he turned over and over in his mind the most puzzling features of his brake problem. In the midst of his meditations he became vaguely conscious of the presence of some one close to his elbow. Whoever it was had apparently been standing there some time. Looking up suddenly, his eyes encountered those of a young woman whom he now recalled having noticed when she entered the office, with a somewhat older companion, just after the noon whistle blew. In her hand she carried a brown-covered pamphlet that looked like a magazine. She held this toward him at once.

"I am trying to raise a little money," she explained, "by taking subscriptions for the *Living Age*. May I show it to you?"

"No, I never read magazines," he answered, waving her away.

"I thought, maybe — " she ventured timidly.

"Try some of those fellows over there," he interrupted, motioning toward a table around which four or five young men were gathered in conversation.

"I have tried them," pleaded the girl, "but they all put me off in the same way. It is discouraging." And in response to a beckoning touch from her companion she started slowly toward the door. Something in her gentle appearance and manner moved him to repent a little of his brusqueness, and he reached out for the magazine she had proffered him. Opening it at random, and passing over a few pages of fiction and miscellaneous essays, his eye was caught by an article entitled "In the Mont Cenis Tunnel." It looked interesting.

"What are you trying to earn money for?" he inquired.

"I am studying to be a teacher," she said, "and I haven't the means to finish my course. I didn't know what else to do, so I took an agency for the magazine in the hope — "

"How far will this go toward a subscription?" he interrupted again. He had fished a bank note from his pocket.

"Two dollars? That will pay for three months."

With a smile, he put down his signature and address in her order-book. She hesitated, and held out her hand.

"My magazine, please. It's my only sample copy."

"Well, begin my subscription with that number. There's something in it I want to read."

She promised and withdrew. He never saw her again, to his knowledge; but their brief interview was to have momentous consequences.

The magazine came in due time; in the interval, other matters had become pressing, and it lay unopened for a few days among his papers at home. Then, one evening, having an hour to spare, he picked it up and turned to the article which had first attracted his attention. The author, a recent visitor to the Mont Cenis tunnel, then in course of construction, described in picturesque phrases the mountain chain, the surrounding country, the approaches. All very well, of course, but what Westinghouse wanted came further on. The engineers in charge, he read, had first considered following the usual practice of sinking vertical shafts or wells from the upper surface at convenient distances apart, and cutting through horizontally from one of these to another; but all the shafts would have been of enormous depth, and one of them, it was estimated, would have required nearly forty years to bore, so that plan had to be abandoned, and the tunnel opened from its opposite ends, the respective gangs working their way toward each other. If they did this by hand, fifty or sixty years must pass before they could meet in the heart of the mountain. Steam machinery might be used for boring; but steam requires fire, and fire feeds on air, and when a gang of laborers had penetrated three miles into the bowels of the earth they would need all the air they could get for their own lungs.

An English engineer had invented an apparatus

which by steam power would drive a drill like a battering-ram against the face of the rock and make holes for blasting. About the same time three Italian engineers, who had been experimenting with compressed air as a motor for driving a railway train up a steep incline in the Apennines, conceived the idea that the combination of the air motor with the drilling machine would solve the tunnel-boring problem. The power would cost nothing, and, instead of consuming air, would supply it to the workmen. "The result," the article continued, "has been a perforating machine, moved by common air compressed to one sixth its natural bulk, and consequently, when set free, exercising an expansive force equal to six atmospheres."

With a triumphant ejaculation, Westinghouse sprang from his chair, and threw the open magazine down on the table. At last he had the answer to his riddle! If compressed air could be conveyed through three thousand feet of pipe and yet retain enough efficiency to drive a drill through the solid stone heart of a mountain chain, it could certainly be carried the length of a railroad train and still exert the force required to set the brakes on the hindmost car. The discovery was his last waking thought that night, and the first thing to welcome his returning consciousness the next morning; and at once he began making working drawings of the machinery necessary for his purpose.

His brief encounter with the Chicago inventor had taught our young friend prudence, and he scrupulously kept his own counsel on the new turn he was taking. He still went on his travels from time to time to sell his earlier inventions; but it had become plain that for the present there was little more money to be made from his reversible frog. This was not because the frog was not as useful as ever, but, since it was made of cast steel, it was so durable that the roads rarely renewed their supply. His partners became restless under the prospect of reduced income, and, after proposing one and another impracticable scheme for cutting down expenses, they summoned him to a confidential council one day, announcing that they had a matter of grave importance to call up.

It was a dismal afternoon when the three men met in the little wooden house which they had adopted as headquarters for their business. The sky, shrouded in dark, threatening clouds, and a cold rain, swept by heavy gusts of wind against the grimy window panes and keeping up a constant fusillade on the roof, united to make a theatrical setting for the scene which followed. Westinghouse was scarcely more than a boy. His partners were men of mature years, recognized in the community as persons of substance. After a few minutes' general discussion of the way sales had declined and the reasons therefor, one of the older men broached the topic which had inspired their desire for a meeting.

"The business," said he, "has become too small for three partners. As two of us have furnished all the capital, while the third has put in merely his time, it seems the logical thing to split right on that line. In other words, you" — addressing Westinghouse — "should either buy us out, or else retire and turn over the whole thing to us."

. The young inventor's indignation was stirred by this summary treatment.

"You know very well," he answered, "that I am in no position to buy you out, so what's the use of talking about that?"

"Well," the other reminded him, "we left open an alternative."

"If I retire, what do you propose to pay me for my patents?"

"Nothing. You have had the use of our money from the start, in return for your services as salesman. If necessary, we can hire an outside traveling man to take your place, and lay him off when trade is dull."

By this time George was worked up to a fine fit of temper.

"So you expect me to make you a present of my patent rights?" he cried "Well, you have missed your guess, for I don't intend to. We'll break up this business here and now, if you say so; but from the moment you and I part company, you make no further use of my patents without paying me as you would a stranger!"

"We'll see!" sneered the spokesman for the other side.

"We will!" retorted George, hotly, as he buttoned his overcoat about him and strode out into the storm.

The two older men had been prepared for a rather trying interview with their youthful partner, but had not counted on his ending it in this defiant style. With a bride to support and no visible means with which to do it, they had looked to see him surrender at discretion. Probably they would have been still more astonished had they heard him, at his father's table that evening, announce his intention of going to Pittsburgh.

"How long shall you be away?" asked his mother.

"I don't know — perhaps I'll stay there, if I like it," said George.

This note of confidence delighted his young wife, who declared that nothing would please her better than to live in Pittsburgh, which she had heard was a growing city and interesting. Then George explained that, a few weeks ago, he had learned of a steel-making plant in Pittsburgh which, with its superior facilities, could unquestionably make his replacement apparatus much cheaper than it could be made in mills nearer home, and he had been in correspondence with the concern on the subject, with the intention of laying the matter before his partners as soon as there were definite data to report. Now he was absolved from any obligation to them and could go ahead on his sole responsibility.

He made his journey according to program, with the purpose of arranging for the firm of Anderson and Cook to manufacture the replacer at their own cost and employ him as a traveling salesman. Never having been in Pittsburgh before, he left his luggage at the station on his arrival, and started out to find his way to the office of the firm, which, his notebook told him, was at the corner of Second Avenue and Try Street. He was slowly walking away from the station, hoping to discover some signs to guide him, when he saw coming toward him a young man of about his own age, tall, good-looking, and well dressed. The stranger espied him at the same moment, and the attraction seemed to be mutual, for they halted, facing each other. Westinghouse explained where he wished to go, and inquired the way. The young man not only pointed it out, but volunteered to go along for a short distance. In a few minutes they had exchanged names, and were chatting like old friends.

The stranger, it appeared, was Ralph Baggaley, a member of one of the most prominent families in Pittsburgh, and the general manager of a local foundry. He had received a part of his education in Germany, and took a keen interest in technical matters. Thus guided, Westinghouse presently found himself at the office of Anderson and Cook, and closeted with the senior partner, who soon arranged with him to start on the road at once and solicit orders from the railroad companies.

Of this opportunity Westinghouse made the most. He filed immediately in the Patent Office at Washington a caveat on his air brake; and from that day forward every railroad officer with whom he discussed the replacer and frog was required later to listen to an exposition of the brake. It was uphill work. One would feign attention, perhaps, only to show by his questions at the end of the monologue that he had not grasped more than half that his caller had been saying. Another would excuse himself for lack of time before the talk had proceeded far. Among those approached was "Commodore" Cornelius Vanderbilt, who proved a good-enough listener, but then, in the direct manner for which he was famous, dismissed the whole project as too imaginative for serious consideration.

From time to time, Westinghouse would return to Pittsburgh to report progress with his sales.   On one of these visits he encountered Baggaley again, and, after an evening's exchange of experiences and opinions, confided to him the air brake scheme. Baggaley was polite, but by no means enthusiastic; it was plain that, in spite of his friendship for the inventor, he regarded the invention as ingenious but visionary.   As Westinghouse warmed to his theme, however, and grew not only eloquent, but convincing in his reasoning, Baggaley became infected with his spirit and began to conjure up in his own mind the great possibilities of the device.   As he was leaving he said · "Westinghouse, we must lose no time in putting this thing before some of the big men in the railroad world."

The other's face fell.

"I could launch it without much difficulty," said he, "if I had a little capital.   I have seen several railroad men already.   They have no way of answering my arguments about the value of the invention if it will work, but I haven't found one yet who was willing to stand the expense of giving it a trial."

"Then a man who has money to risk would be of more use to you just now than one who knows railroading?"

"That's it."

"Perhaps your father would help you now, if you put the case before him in that way."

Once more George approached his father in the hope of inducing him to buy a fractional interest in the patent; but, in the correspondence which followed, Mr. Westinghouse manifested more strongly than ever his distaste for what he still regarded as a pure speculation.

CHAPTER V

Doubt Changed to Certainty

In spite of his air of confidence, Westinghouse had begun to wonder, after his series of rebuffs, whether there might not be some technical feature of his invention which made men of broader training and experience than his suspicious of it. None of them had suggested such a thing, though he had given them plenty of openings; possibly, he reflected, they were too considerate of his feelings to tell him the truth to his face. He resolved therefore to obtain one verdict on which he could depend as unbiased even by courtesy. Baggaley had announced an intention to back the venture with a few thousand dollars he was able to command, so that they could be prepared to take instant advantage of any proposal that might suddenly come to them for an experiment; but Westinghouse was reluctant to let his friend assume such a risk till both felt sure that they were on solid ground.

"We are wasting time with so much hesitation," declared Baggaley one day. "Let me put all the drawings, directions, and claims into the hands of a man I know, the most highly skilled mechanical expert in the city of Pittsburgh, and have him pass on them.   It will cost something, for he gets good fees for his opinions, but I think it will pay in the end."

Westinghouse consenting, this was done.   The expert gave the subject his careful scrutiny, and in the course of a fortnight handed back a written opinion, which his young client read with feverish eagerness.   It was a sweeping condemnation of the whole scheme as not only unsound but nonsensical. Baggaley hurried with the paper to Westinghouse, who went over it twice before handing it back.   The rising color in his face showed that he was angry, but he gave no immediate vent to his feelings.

"How much did your expert charge you for that death sentence?" he asked, after a little.

"One hundred dollars."

"Well, what are you going to do about it?"

"Watch me and see."   And Baggaley, setting his teeth hard, tore the manuscript into ribbons and threw it into the grate.   As it did not catch at once, he struck a match and lighted the little pile, standing over it till the last fragment of paper had been turned into ashes, and the smoke from it had disappeared up the chimney.

"That's a nice way to treat an expert's report," remarked Westinghouse with grim humor, as he followed the other's motions with his eyes.   "Apparently you don't consider the fellow's opinion worth so much now as you did before you got it?"

"It was worth the hundred dollars I paid for it — every cent: it has taught me a lesson that I could not have bought otherwise for ten times the money.

Hereafter I back my own judgment and let outsiders go. George, I'll put up your common sense against the special education of any expert in Christendom ! Now let's get to work, so as to be ready for the show that somebody is sure to give us soon."

Both took fresh heart and plunged in with a will. Although it was an expensive undertaking, Westinghouse, with Baggaley's support, prepared the apparatus for an experiment as elaborately as if they had a train of cars already at the door, waiting to be equipped. But even the railroad managers to whom the subject was presented in its new light were disposed to fight shy of it. Their rolling-stock was already supplied with brakes, they argued, and, while it was always possible that something better than they had might come along, they felt that, if they had procured the best outfit at that time in general use, they had done their duty to the public, and spent as much of their stockholders' money as they had a right to. Now and then one would concede a half-promise that he would lay the question before his directors at their next meeting; but either he failed to do so, or the directors declined to look into it, and the weeks slipped by till the autumn of 1868 was at hand. In the meantime Westinghouse had brought his wife from Schenectady, and they had established themselves in Pittsburgh in a very modest way.

Then came upon the scene Robert Pitcairn, local superintendent of the Pennsylvania Railroad, who promptly took a strong fancy to Westinghouse. After lending a sympathetic ear to the usual explanation of the brake and prophecies of its future importance, "If I can get my people interested," said he, "I believe there is enough in the invention to be worth a fair trial."

The flagging hopes of the young men sprang up with a bound. A few days later, at Mr. Pitcairn's instigation, Superintendent Williams came on from Altoona accompanied by Andrew J. Cassatt, then assistant superintendent of motive power for the company and already recognized as one of its coming notables. The two looked the apparatus over with great particularity, and interrogated its sponsors with an intelligence no one else except Mr. Pitcairn had thus far displayed. This carried the matter a stage further than anything that had preceded it; they were frank enough to say that they regarded the invention as having more than ordinary merit, but — and here followed the old, familiar reaction — they were not prepared to recommend that their company shoulder the entire expense of a practical demonstration. Could not the young men arrange to bear this, provided the company would furnish the track and the train, the engineer and the crew, free of charge?

No, the young men did not see their way clear to do so. They were sorry, but, in constructing a complete equipment for a locomotive and one car, they had already gone to as heavy expense as they felt justified in incurring. Could not the company meet them on a little more advantageous ground? Mr. Cassatt and his companion expressed their serious doubts. If they could individually do just what they wished to without consulting any one else, they would be entirely willing to offer more liberal terms for the sake of an experiment.   The most they could do was to promise that they would think everything over conscientiously and make a perfectly well-balanced report, but they would hold out no encouragement to look for a more favorable decision from headquarters.

In the midst of the brief depression which followed this rapid rise and fall of his anticipations, Westinghouse received one day an unheralded visit from Superintendent W. W. Card of the Steubenville division of the Panhandle Railroad.

"I understand," said he, "that you have invented a remarkable brake?"

Westinghouse, hardly able to trust his ears, assured Mr. Card that this was the fact, and proceeded to expatiate on the special excellences of his invention. Instead of the polite repression he had learned to expect from railroad officers when he opened his floodgates of panegyric, he met with incitements to go on from one point to another.   And not only that, but his extraordinary visitor, after listening attentively to all he had to say, examined the sample apparatus, part by part, with an appraising eye, accompanying the inspection with comments which showed that not a word of the explanation had been lost upon him.

"If this will do all it appears capable of," was his summing-up, as he surveyed the mechanism once more in perspective, "you have opened a gold mine, Mr. Westinghouse.   The railroads have been waiting a long time for a really good brake. What we have now will answer only so long as we can find nothing better in the market. When the right one comes along, it will find the roads all ready for it."

A few days later he called again, bringing with him the purchasing agent of his company, who was as much impressed as he had been with the promise the new device held forth; but, in spite of Card's urgent appeal that he order an experimental outfit and make a practical test at the company's cost, the agent declined, on the ground that he dared not take so material a step without authority from the directors. He would, he added, go before the board with Mr. Card and put the case to them as strongly as he could.

He was as good as his word. The directors, however, balked at the proposed outlay, and the net result of the whole negotiation was a written order from the president of the company, Thomas L. Jewett, that the use of a train for a trial trip be placed at the disposal of the inventor, conditioned on the latter's contracting to equip it at his own expense and to reimburse the company for any damage done to locomotive or cars by the attachment of the apparatus.

This was no better, really, than the Pitcairn-Cassatt proposal, but the young men were tired of alternate hopes and disappointments, and grasped at it rather than wait longer. They differed only on one point. Westinghouse, with his fervid imagination in full action, was willing to run into almost any debt for the money needed to get ready; Baggaley, who had had some experience in handling funds, insisted that they must keep every expenditure down to the lowest practicable figure. With what they had already done in the way of building a specimen brake apparatus, it took them a comparatively short time to complete their preparations, and on the day appointed they had on hand their air pump, their main reservoir for the locomotive, cylinders for four cars — the maximum length of the accommodation train on which the test was to be made — and the piping and hose connections required to connect the locomotive reservoir with the car cylinders. On the morning fixed for the trial trip, the rear car of the train was reserved for a party of invited guests, including those officers of the Panhandle company who were not too timid to risk life and limb with an untried device, and a few magnates of other companies who seemed to have an open mind on the subject of the new brake.

Daniel Tate, the engineer, was a bright young fellow, and it did not take Westinghouse a great while to give him the final instructions about the brake so that he felt perfectly confident of his ability to make it work. Westinghouse, as he descended from the cab, grasped Tate's hand and wrung it with warmth.

"All I ask of you, Dan," said he earnestly, "is to give this thing a fair show. Good luck to you!"

Dan nodded a promise, and reached for his bell rope. As he did so, something dropped from his hand, the one Westinghouse had been shaking. It was a little paper wad, which, when he had picked it up and smoothed it out, proved to be a fifty-dollar note. Acting on quick impulse to restore what he feared was lost money, he leaned out of the cab and looked down the train; Westinghouse was just boarding the hindmost car. Their eyes met, and Tate held up the bill. Westinghouse smiled, but motioned him to put it into his pocket. Tate did so, well pleased with the generosity of the gift, but little suspecting that it contained the last dollar the young man had in purse or in prospect.

Within a short distance of the Panhandle station was a tunnel about one sixth of a mile long, piercing Grant Hill and emerging at Fourth Avenue, where accommodation trains were accustomed to halt to pick up passengers. As this trial train was not to stop there, Tate rapidly increased its speed till it was moving at the rate of about thirty miles an hour. Abundant precaution was supposed to have been taken to prevent pedestrians or vehicles from getting upon the track at the two surface crossings between there and the bridge spanning the Monongahela River, beyond which the Panhandle ran into the open country. But, of course, "a fool there was" in the person of a drayman on Second Avenue who disregarded all warnings and pushed ahead till, as his horses stepped into the space between the rails, he saw bearing down upon him, only two blocks away, the big, black front of a locomotive. It was too late to pull back, and in a frenzy of terror he laid the lash with all his might over the animals' flanks. The horses were as badly demoralized as he, and their first response was to plunge forward with a motion which loosened the crosswise plank he was using for a seat, and threw him to the ground with his body across one of the rails.

The whole thing had happened in barely an instant of time, and a tragedy was averted only by the quick wit of the engineer. Tate, who had just been turning over in his mind the most effective way of bringing the train to a standstill at the first station where it was to halt, reached instinctively for the brake valve and gave it a mighty twist. The air rushed out of the compressor through the pipes into the cylinders beneath the cars, and the pistons brought the brake shoes with force against the wheels. There was a grating sound and a sudden jar as the train came to a stop with the cowcatcher of the locomotive only four feet on the safe side of the unhappy driver.

In the flash of an eye Tate had swung himself out of the cab and was helping the man to his feet. Then, leaving his fireman in charge of the engine, he ran back to see how the stop had affected the train generally. He was met by Westinghouse and a number of the invited guests, most of whom were rubbing their heads or their shins, or pressing their battered hats into shape as they limped along. Every one was eager to know what the matter was, and the pleasure of all at learning that the spasmodic application of the brakes had saved a human life, was a salve to the discomfort they had suffered from being hurled without warning out of their seats and strewn over the floor of their car, which, as the tail of the train, had received the worst shock. When they had first alighted they had been almost in fighting mood; but as they climbed back the general verdict was that the air brake was capable of doing what its inventor claimed for it. A question was raised whether, having witnessed such a demonstration, they should reverse the train and return to Pittsburgh; but the proposal was unanimously voted down, and the whole party proceeded to Steubenville as originally planned. Tate treated them, on the way, to several tests which were as satisfying, even if not quite so drastic, as the initial one. He was as pleased with the apparatus as a child with a new toy, and took the utmost pride in showing how easily, and with what varied effects, it could be handled.

When the return trip was ended, Westinghouse, full of elation over his triumph, shook hands with his guests and started for home to tell his wife the news. But before he got many steps away from the station he paused and reëntered it, hastening to the telegraph office, where he filed the following despatch to his father in Schenectady:

" My air brake had practical trial today on passenger train on Panhandle Railroad and proved a great success. GEORGE."

He was still sanguine enough to hope that, in the face of such a fulfillment of prophecy, the old gentleman would experience a change of heart and volunteer an offer to finance the next stage of the business. But nothing of the sort was forthcoming. Mr. Westinghouse was evidently in no haste to make a princely fortune. His only response to the telegram was a short and characteristic letter expressing in prudent phraseology his pleasure at reading so favorable a report, and remarking that, the brake having already "proved a great success," of course there would be no further difficulty in procuring all the money needed for manufacturing and marketing it.

The first air brake patent was issued to Westinghouse on the thirteenth of April, 1869. But meanwhile he had not been idle. Feeling that he now could afford to resign his place as salesman for Anderson and Cook and devote his entire time to the promotion of his new enterprise, he laid certain plans before Baggaley, who gladly joined forces with him. The firm with which Baggaley had been connected was dissolved, and its foundry was converted temporarily into a plant for the manufacture of air brakes. Some of the leading officers of the Pennsylvania Railroad Company, having recovered from their first apathy and being anxious to make up for lost time, fitted out an exhibition train to run to Altoona, primarily to show the working of the new brake to the directors of their corporation, but incidentally to perform an important service in publicity. A number of newspaper writers were taken along, and in a few days the press everywhere was furnished with the story of the invention.

In Philadelphia, Westinghouse used the same train for demonstration purposes, with many prominent railroad men from various parts of the country as witnesses; among the rest was the general superintendent of the Chicago and Northwestern system, who was so impressed with what he saw that he invited the inventor to bring the train to Chicago and

The First Westinghouse Air Brake Factory

exhibit it.   This was done, with the effect of introducing the brake to the notice of a number of Western railroad managers who had not yet seen it work. From Chicago Westinghouse was invited to St. Louis, where the same thing was repeated.   From that point the brake made its own way without the expenditure of any extraordinary effort, and orders began to come in from quarters where the inventor had but recently seen only the cold shoulder turned toward his advances.

In July, 1869, the Westinghouse Air Brake Company was organized under a Pennsylvania charter with a capitalization of five hundred thousand dollars. In these days when we talk of all considerable enterprises in terms of millions, this seems like a modest start, but measured by the standards of half a century ago it was regarded as a very heavy responsibility for a comparative youth of unknown antecedents to shoulder.   The board of directors was wisely chosen from among the group of men who were familiar with the air brake mechanism and had witnessed the experimental tests of its efficiency, and whose names, for the most part, stood for something in the railroad world.   These were Robert Pitcairn, W. W. Card, Andrew J. Cassatt, Edward H. Williams, G. D. Whitcomb, Ralph Baggaley, and, of course, Westinghouse, who became first president of the corporation.   John Caldwell was elected treasurer.

Everything seemed to be moving along as satisfactorily as could be hoped, when the directors, at one of their meetings, were treated to a shock.   A patent expert whom they had engaged to go through all the railway brake literature of this and other countries, and ascertain for them just what relation the Westinghouse invention bore to previous essays in the same field, brought in a report that, about thirty years before, essentially the same device had been patented in England, but proved so unpractical that the patent expired before any use had been made of it. The consternation which reigned for a little while was dispelled when Westinghouse, by an analysis of the terms of the British patent, showed that the mechanism it covered was unworkable in emergencies because, before the brake could be applied, the locomotive driver was required to turn steam into a pump for compressing the air, whereas his own apparatus had the air already stored in a compressor on the locomotive.

The discomforting suggestion conveyed in the report, however, promptly bore good fruit; for the always lively imagination of young Westinghouse was spurred by it to the question · "If the English railways are still unequipped with a first-rate air brake, why not sell them mine?" As usual with him, action was quick to follow thought. The Pittsburgh works had got well under way during the winter of 1869 and 1870, and by the autumn of the latter year he was ready for his invasion of the old world. Although he took his wife with him, it cost him something of a wrench to cut loose from the scene of his first large activities, for he had recently bought a house and lot at Homewood, on the eastern edge of the city, christened the little estate "Solitude", and settled down to his first real experience as lord of a domestic establishment.   But if he were made a trifle homesick by the prospect of leaving everything on which he had fixed his heart's desire on this side of the water he felt more so when he reached the other side and found himself in the chilliest atmosphere he had ever encountered.

CHAPTER VI

"Nothing Succeeds Like Success"

Americans who know England and the English only on the hospitable side they present to our country and its people today will have some difficulty in appreciating the situation existing when George Westinghouse made his first entry into London. Up to that time there had not been established any of the reciprocity of cordial sentiment which has characterized the intercourse of the two nations during the last twenty years. On our part, we were still cherishing the hostile traditions of 1776 and 1812, and resentful memories of the privateering episodes of the early '60's; on theirs, there was a sense of rancor at our encouragement, for political purposes, of Irish insurgency and almost everything else that was notoriously anti-English. Moreover, in those days, whatever was associated with American railroading was under more or less suspicion in England, owing to several well-advertised misfortunes suffered by English investors in wildcat projects here. The era of corporate inflation opened by our Civil War, the launching of the first crude schemes for transcontinental rail routes, the abuse of the Erie system as a football of professional stock gamblers, and the struggle continually going on between rival specu-

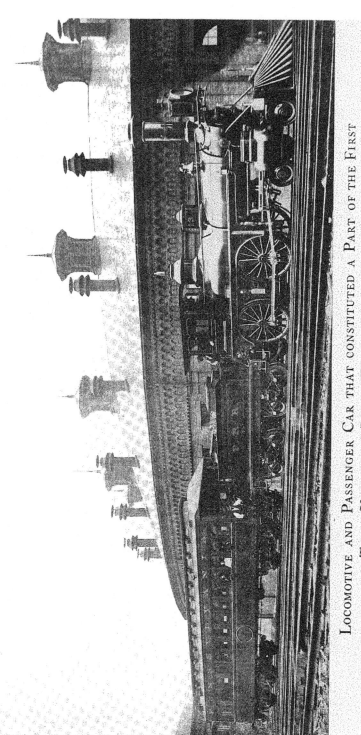

LOCOMOTIVE AND PASSENGER CAR THAT CONSTITUTED A PART OF THE FIRST
TRAIN USED FOR A PUBLIC EXHIBITION OF THE BRAKE

This train was taken to Chicago, St. Louis and Philadelphia for test purposes

lative rings for the control of a few valuable properties
for questionable purposes had combined to give the
more conservative element in English business circles
a notion of American affairs generally as disagreeable
as it was unjust.

In view of these conditions, it appeared to Westinghouse a wise precaution to ascertain the feeling
of the scientific periodicals toward such an invention
as his before attempting to place it in the hands of
any of the carrying companies. He made overtures
in one or two quarters where, as soon as he announced
his nationality, he met with a repulse. The last
journal he approached was *Engineering*, a weekly
which he had seen now and then at home, where its
original editor, Zerah Colburn, was well known.
Two editors had since succeeded Mr. Colburn —
Messrs. W. H. Maw and J. Dredge. It so happened
that when he made his first call Mr. Maw was out
of the office, and he was received by Mr. Dredge,
who seemed, in spite of the customary English reserve, to take an instant liking to him. In a few
minutes Westinghouse was deep in his exposition of
his air brake. Dredge listened curiously, but gave
him no immediate sign of encouragement. At the
close of their talk, Westinghouse left with the editor
a copy of his patent, with some additional drawings
and a popular description prepared by himself.
Mr. Dredge consented to examine the documents
carefully as soon as he could command the necessary
time, and, if he found them satisfactory, to publish
his impressions.

"But I warn you, Mr. Westinghouse," he said

good-naturedly, as he fastened the folio and laid it
among his more important papers, "you have put
your head into the lion's mouth, and will have no
one but yourself to blame if it is bitten off."

"I'll take my chances," laughed Westinghouse.
"Of course, it makes a world of difference if you know
the habits of your lion."

The whimsical challenge, though taken up so
blithely on the spot, recurred to the inventor's mind
several times between this interview and the appearance of the next issue of *Engineering*, through which
he looked in vain for any comment on his brake.
Every time he thought of it, it had taken on a little
more serious significance, till he had begun to wonder
whether he might not, after all, have made a mistake
in coming to a periodical of so high standing before
making a practical test of his brake somewhere in
Great Britain.   The notion was strengthened when,
after a considerable interval, he called upon Mr.
Dredge again, to inquire what prospect there was of
an article at an early date.   The editor handed him
a sheet of proof to read, with the remark: "I have
been favorably impressed with your brake, from the
literature about it which you left me.   I am keeping
that for future use if an occasion offers itself.   Just
now, however, the thing for you to do is to place your
brake on one of our railways and give a public exhibition of its working.   The readers of *Engineering*
will take far more interest in a statement of what we
have seen with our own eyes than in any suggestion
we might print, founded on nothing more substantial
than your patent and claims."

"My brake," argued Westinghouse, "is already in constant use on several American roads."

"Doubtless," assented Dredge; "and yet you will appreciate the fact that our people are a bit skeptical about the operations of American railways unless they have evidence of a very convincing character."

"What do you wish? Shall I give you a list of the roads in the United States which use my brake, and let you write to the managers and learn for yourself whether my pretensions are justified?"

"That's not a bad idea. Incidentally, however, I have put into your hands the rough draft of something I shall say in *Engineering* apropos of the general subject of air brakes. If your invention proves to be all that you say it is, this demand of mine will make a very good form of introduction for what I may wish to write later. Mind you, I am not saying that all you claim may not be absolutely well founded. I merely intend to take reasonable means of assuring myself."

Westinghouse withdrew, bearing with him Dredge's proof sheet, which he read with interest at the first opportunity. It was a broad plea for a better brake than any then in use on British railways, and it gave a catalogue of the qualities which the editor considered essential to a satisfactory continuous braking system for trains, about as follows:

First, the brakes must be applicable with equal facility by either the locomotive-driver or the guards who might be in various parts of a train;

Second, the act of applying the brakes must call

for only a slight exertion on the. part of the person performing it;

Third, the application must be capable of either instantaneous or gradual performance, according to the peculiar character of the exigency;

Fourth, if a part of the train breaks loose from the rest, the brakes must come automatically into play;

Fifth, the system must permit carriages, whether fitted with the brakes or not, to be attached to, or detached from, the train;

Sixth, when a train is divided, the brakes on every division must be capable of working independently;

Seventh, the failure of the brake apparatus on one or more carriages must not interfere with the action of the brakes on the rest of the train;

Eighth, the brake mechanism must be of very simple character, easy to maintain, and not liable to derangement by rough use, or disuse and neglect.

At a first reading, these conditions struck Westinghouse as rather severe, but he was cheerfulness itself when next he called upon Dredge and offered to return the borrowed proof.

"Oh, keep it, if it interests you," said the editor, with a wave of the hand. "Are you prepared now to tell me that your brake meets all my requirements?"

"By no means," answered Westinghouse "But it is still in its infancy, and I am quite certain that before I get through with it you will have no fault to find with its operation."

"You are still working on it?"

"I don't suppose I shall ever stop."

"By Jove!" Dredge brought his flat palm down upon a pile of papers before him. "You speak like a man of spirit. I like that. Although you are an inventor, you're not blinded by your own genius."

"No, I can still see well enough to discover the faults in your catalogue of requisites."

"For example — ?" the editor was all attention.

"For a first criticism, you are indiscriminate. You apparently recognize no distinction between the needs of a train making long runs and one that has a short route and stops every few minutes — what we call in America an 'accommodation.' Don't you see that the chances are all against having to divide a train, attach and detach cars, and so forth where the stations are only eight or ten miles apart at most?"

"That is a fair criticism as far as it goes." Dredge made a few notes in pencil on a memorandum sheet. "What next?"

"Why, perhaps I should take an exception also to your fourth demand, when applied to local trains. With fast running, there is always the liability that a coupling may break under the strain, and your train be cut in two; whereas, at any speed ever reached between stations almost within gunshot of each other, the possibility of such an accident is reduced to a minimum."

"Nevertheless, you admit that it exists?"

"Of course. But don't you see that the forward fragment of your train would reach the next station so soon that there would really be no danger to life or property before the missing part could be picked up and reattached?"

"There it is! You Americans are always calculating probabilities — taking chances."

"And you Britishers go to the other extreme, which is just as bad, or worse. I wonder you ever dare lay out a program for tomorrow; who knows that it will come?"

Dredge, so far from being nettled by the retort, chuckled audibly.

"Very well, Young America, I've made a note of your criticisms and will give them due consideration. I still stand by my first proposition, however, that *Engineering* had better wait until you have placed your brake on an experimental train in this country, as you did at the start in the United States. Then, whatever we print will have weight."

There being nothing left to discuss, Westinghouse took his leave, and the next morning entered upon a systematic campaign among the railway companies. He had brought with him, from men of standing in the transportation business in America, letters of introduction to some of their English brethren; but in spite of such an armament he found it no easy matter to pierce the wall of form and ceremony with which these magnates had surrounded themselves. As illustrative of the common attitude, he used to enjoy, later in life, telling the story of his visit to the managing director of one great railway, whom he asked, by way of opening conversation, whether he had read a little pamphlet that had been mailed him a few days before, descriptive of the new brake.

"No," was the frigid response. "I receive many pamphlets in my mail, but I rarely read them."

"Neither do I," said Westinghouse; "most of them would not pay me for my time. But as this one contains information about a new thing in your special field — "

"So many new things," interrupted the manager, "are worthless, that as a rule they have ceased to interest me."

"Well, here is one which will, I am sure." Westinghouse drew a duplicate from his pocket. "With your permission, I will give you a brief abstract of its contents." And he plunged, as he had so often while his invention was still untried, into a recitation of its points of especial merit, concluding his speech with an account of the actual tests it had met so creditably on American railroads. At the close of his exposition he asked permission to equip a locomotive, tender and car on this gentleman's road, and prove beyond question what the apparatus could do.

"Let you use *our* property for such a purpose?" ejaculated the astounded manager. "I really could not think of it for a moment!"

"But I am ready to attach my apparatus at my own expense," pleaded the visitor.

"Oh, quite so, quite so; I take that for granted. It makes no difference, however. We have not a locomotive, a tender or a carriage to spare for your experiments."

"Then could I not hire the necessary vehicles, equip them with my brake, and give an exhibition in the presence of any number of gentlemen you care to invite?"

"No, no. You positively must take my refusal as final. In the plainest terms, we do not wish to rent any of our rolling stock for you to use in your demonstration." By this time the railroad man's manner was very impatient, and his face was growing purple. In spite of so threatening a symptom the inventor persisted.

"Possibly you will consent, then, to *sell* me a train? All I really need is a locomotive, a tender and four passenger coaches. What is your price for such an outfit over here?"

If this irrepressible young Yankee had struck him with a bludgeon, the Englishman could hardly have appeared more dazed. It took him a full minute to realize what he had heard, and to make sure that his visitor was in earnest, before he answered:

"You will have to give me a little time to consider that question. It is too extraordinary to be settled in an instant. I can probably give you an answer in about a week. But I assume you understand that, even if we consent to sell you a train, such a concession would not include permission to run over our tracks with your machinery. We must stop short of that, you know."

Rising with a bow which announced as distinctly as words that the interview was at an end, the man of fifty dismissed the youth of twenty-five quite without a thought that the next time they met for a negotiation the man would be making the bid and the youth taking time to consider it.

But this is what happened, though it was a good while in coming. In March, 1872, the London and North-Western Railway Company gave Westinghouse permission to exhibit his brake on its line between Stafford and Crewe, and, about the same time, he was allowed to equip a train of twelve passenger coaches and two freight cars for a series of tests on the Caledonian Railway between Glasgow and Wemyss Bay. In each instance the demonstration was successful. A little later several trials were made on the South-Eastern Railway with a train consisting of a locomotive, tender, and six cars, and the witnesses were free with their praise of the way the apparatus acted. Still, neither these corporations, nor any others whose representatives were present at the tests, were willing to prove their satisfaction at once by formally adopting the Westinghouse brake as their standard. The first real step forward was taken by the Metropolitan District Railway in London in January, 1873. Eighteen months afterward the British Board of Trade conducted a series of brake trials in which chain, hydraulic, and vacuum brakes competed with the air brake. In 1875 another series of tests was made under the auspices of the British Railways Accident Commission. In all these the Westinghouse proved itself the most efficient continuous brake on the market. Everybody except the vacuum brake manufacturers seemed willing to concede its superiority, but many of the railroad managers complained that it was too expensive. This brought *Engineering* again to the fore with evidence gathered from a host of American experts that the original cost of equipping their lines with Westinghouse brakes was more than made up by the saving on repairs.

At first Westinghouse had fancied that the reluctance manifested in England to accepting his brake outright might be due to the local railways having already some sufficiently good apparatus of which he had not learned.   To see for himself the actual conditions, he engaged a man familiar with local railway operations to travel with him throughout Great Britain.   Speaking afterward of these trips he said : "I found that there were no continuous brakes in use except on a few trains on the London and North-Western and the North London railways.   These were fitted with Clark's chain brakes, operated by a guard from the brake van, and not connected or attached to the locomotive.   I failed to find a single continuous brake in which power was communicated throughout the train through lines of pipe, except what was known as Barker's hydraulic system, which was then in process of trial.   There never had been any compressed air brakes in successful operation in England.   The London, Chatham, and Dover Railway had tried one on a train running between the Crystal Palace and Victoria station, but had abandoned it as unsatisfactory;   and the locomotive superintendent of the Great Northern Railway had had some sort of experience with one which convinced him that the underlying principle was impracticable, so that for a long time I could not obtain even a hearing in that quarter.   With these exceptions I could find no evidence that air brakes of any kind had ever even been tried."

Not all the period covered by this outline was passed continuously in England.   Between 1871 and 1881 Westinghouse crossed the ocean repeatedly, keeping thus in close touch with his American company. He also made several fruitful visits to the Continental capitals, where the air brake met with a much warmer reception than among English railway managers. In Belgium, for example, a royal commission of engineers, after a thorough comparison of his brake with all others which had been brought to their attention, adopted it as the standard equipment for the state railways; and from other sources there gradually came limited orders which, though obviously only experimental, gave him a feeling that his invention was making its way in the old world in spite of its apparently unpromising start. To facilitate the handling of his European business, he organized a British corporation and established a large plant for the manufacture of the brake, with executive offices in London. His most formidable competitor was a vacuum brake company; and it is significant of the conservatism bred into the flesh and bone of even the most intelligent class of Englishmen that, though the rest of the world has for the most part adopted the air brake as by far the most satisfactory device yet invented, many of the British railroads are still committed to the vacuum brake and resist all movements for a change.

Meanwhile, instead of resenting criticisms which often were hard to bear, Westinghouse had turned them to profit by studying out the improvements they called for in one and another feature, culminating in the invention of the now familiar automatic brake, which he patented in 1872, and which fulfilled in every respect the ideal requirements proposed by Mr. Dredge. The original non-automatic or "straight-air" brake had consisted of a very simple steam-actuated air pump placed on the side of the locomotive, and a reservoir in which the compressed air could be stored. A pipe line from the reservoir was carried through the length of the train, connections between vehicles being made by means of hose and couplings. Every vehicle was provided with a simple cast-iron cylinder, the piston rod of which was connected with the brake rigging in such a way that when the air was admitted to the cylinder the piston was forced out, and the brakes were thereby applied. In the engineer's cab there was placed in the pipe line a three-way cock, by means of which compressed air could be admitted to the pipe line and thus to the cylinder on every car; or the air already in the cylinders and pipe line could be discharged to the atmosphere, releasing the brakes.

Excellent as this apparatus was by comparison with any predecessor in the same line, it lacked certain desirable features and was liable to prove inoperative in some emergency when it would be most needed, from the bursting of the hose under pressure, the parting of the train or other rupture of the system. In order to obviate such perilous possibilities, Westinghouse brought out what is now known as the automatic brake. Its essential difference from the "straight-air" brake consisted in the installation of supplementary or auxiliary reservoirs for the storage of compressed air on the cars in addition to the main reservoir on the locomotive; thus every vehicle carried its own source of power, and the employment of an ingenious valve mechanism to cause the application of the brake by the reduction of air pressure in the train-pipe — no matter whether the reduction were made intentionally or by accident — so that a ruptured hose or a serious air leakage from whatever source would stop the train. This device was called a "triple valve", because of its threefold function of applying a brake, releasing it, and charging its auxiliary reservoir. As a product of pure invention it is probable that the automatic brake system represented in the highest degree Westinghouse's capacity as an inventor.

It was not merely in large matters that Westinghouse found his progress impeded by insular prejudice during his early British campaign, but in lesser details as well. In a speech he made in London in 1903 before a distinguished body of scientific men, he was able to take a laughing glance backward at these annoyances, time having vindicated his foresight.

"I came here first," said he, "about thirty years ago, and for ten years I was here half my time. At that time it was very difficult to get anything done in England, as I could get no one to believe in anything I proposed. I wanted in those early days to try an iron brake shoe, because, on account of the rapid wear, we could not keep the wooden shoes adjusted. I had to beg and plead to be permitted to put a set of metal brake shoes on one tender of the Caledonian Railway. Finally I succeeded. Of course, you all know that nowadays all the railway brake shoes or blocks are made of cast iron or other metal and are used upon all the wheels of the train."

By the fall of 1881 the Westinghouse automatic air brake was in use on over 3164 locomotives and 17,290 cars in various foreign countries, ranging from over 1087 locomotives and 7719 cars in Great Britain, and 1416 locomotives and 7193 cars in France, down to one locomotive and six cars in Sweden. In the United States, 3435 locomotives and 12,790 cars were equipped with it. Of the fourteen British railways employing it, the largest patrons were the North-Eastern, the London, Brighton, and South Coast, the Great Eastern, the North British, the Caledonian, and the Glasgow and South-Western systems. The statistics, here given, moreover, do not include the straight-air brakes, of which a very large number were still in use on railways which had bought them before the automatic brake came into general notice. As a fitting conclusion to the catalogue of ten years' achievements, Europe was dotted with manufacturing establishments where hundreds of mechanics were busy producing Westinghouse brake apparatus, with a combined capacity for equipping an average of three hundred locomotives and twelve hundred cars every month. And all this had been evolved from the brain and hand of an American just turned thirty-five, who, obliged to hew his own way without the aid of powerful allies, had by sheer energy and pluck already raised himself from obscurity to eminence and a steadily improving bank account.

CHAPTER VII

THE BATTLE OF THE BRAKES

UP to 1880 the use of power brakes was confined wholly to passenger service; but some railroads in the mountainous regions of the West had grades so steep as to render the conduct of their freight traffic very hazardous, and this led to their adopting presently a straight-air brake, and later an automatic brake specially designed for their use. At that time the freight trains on lines west of the Missouri River were comparatively short, and there was little interchange of cars between them, so that every road used the equipment best suited to its needs, practically without reference to the equipment of its neighbors. In the East, however, the length of the trains was continually on the increase, and the interchange of cars was so general that the introduction of power brakes for freight traffic had not yet been attempted. Meanwhile, as trains grew longer and loads heavier, accidents to human life, goods in transit, and rolling stock occurred with more and more frequency, emphasizing the need of some kind of automatic coupling to replace the old link and pin, the substitution of power brakes for hand brakes, and the establishment of a uniform standard of mechanisms in both instances, so that a car of any one line could be inserted in a train of any other and be operated under the same control.

An efficient coupler was finally developed and adopted, but the determination of a standard power brake presented greater difficulties. There were several inventions in the field, and the Master Car Builders' Association decided to clear the situation by designating a committee to conduct a series of competitive tests between them at Burlington, Iowa. The first meet was fixed for the spring of 1886, and, although every brake manufacturer in the country was invited to take part with a train of fifty cars fitted with his own apparatus, this trial was to all intents an elimination contest, since only the automatic air and the vacuum brakes made a showing on which any reasonable hope could be based. The committee reported that the operation of the automatic air brake met the ordinary requirements of service work, but that its action was unsatisfactory in emergencies because of the slow passage of the power from the front to the rear of a long train. With the sudden stoppage from low speeds of such a train, by the application of the brakes with full force, the cars at the front end would come to an almost instant standstill, those further back banging successively into them till the influence exerted from the locomotive had reached the last car. Animals in the cattle cars were liable to be wounded or killed by being hurled into heaps, the forward end of a heavy car might smash the rear end of a light one and ruin everything fragile carried therein, and train hands were in danger of being thrown into the spaces between cars and crushed to death or permanently crippled.

Another trial was accordingly set for the spring of the following year, at the same place. Between the two trials Westinghouse bent his entire thought upon studying out a means of increasing the emergency speed of action of his brake in the parts of the train furthest from the locomotive, and this he accomplished.

Six competitors took part in the fresh test. One brake was operated by electricity alone; a second by compressed air alone; a third by electricity and a vacuum; while Westinghouse and one other manufacturer contributed brakes combining compressed air and electricity. The electric appliances used by Westinghouse were very simple, and not required on every car; two or three of them, inserted between the hose couplings in various parts of a long train, sufficed to produce the desired results. The arrangement was such that when the brakes were set electrically the pneumatic application was made also, and in the event of an electrical failure the train would still be stopped pneumatically; whereas the other electrically-operated brakes had complicated and delicate mechanisms on every car, and if the electric operation failed the engineer lost control of the train. The improvements Westinghouse had recently made in the triple valve conveyed the braking force from the locomotive to the last car on a fifty-car freight train more than twice as quickly as this had ever been done before; yet the lapse of time between the first and final applications was still distinctly measurable, and the enhanced efficiency of the individual brakes increased rather than lessened the shock evil.

In the trials of 1887 an instrument called a slide-ometer was used to determine the relative violence of the shocks produced by sudden stopping under various conditions. It consisted of a wooden trough, fourteen feet long by six inches wide, made of clear white pine smoothly planed. This was screwed fast to the center of the rear car, and in it would slide, in either direction, a wrought iron disc weighing a trifle more than sixteen pounds. Crude as the device appeared, it answered its purpose well. Shocks in the ordinary handling of trains with slack couplings, over sags or hogbacks, or working in yards, would move the disc from two to eight inches; twelve inches indicated a shock sufficient to injure live stock and equipment; while repeated blows registering from twelve to twenty inches would start the loads at the rear of the train through the ends of the cars. It was soon evident that not all the improvement yet made in the automatic air brake had carried it past the danger point, as the sudden stoppage of a train moving at a speed of twenty miles an hour, under some conditions, caused the disc to slide more than one hundred and twenty inches; only when electricity was employed to operate the air valves were the results satisfactory. The committee's report, therefore, was generally favorable to a brake operated by air, having valves actuated by electricity — practically a verdict against brakes operated by air alone.

Among the technically trained observers who attended these trials, probably the only one who did not read in this turn of affairs an end to the dominance of Westinghouse in his special field was Westinghouse himself. To a friend who attempted to say something comforting, he turned a face which, though serious, was entirely cheerful.

"What are you going to do now?" asked the friend.

"What I have left undone hitherto," he answered — "perfect my air brake."

To this task he addressed his attention with the same industry that had characterized his previous undertakings. He felt that the electric factor must be eliminated if possible, because of the perils of depending upon an agency so liable to accident from uncontrollable conditions. As the improved triple valve had proved that it was based on a correct principle, he devoted his first thought to various accessories, of which the details of construction in any wise influenced the flow of air in the apparatus. The ports of the triple valve were also enlarged, and this, with succeeding modifications of kindred nature, enabled him, within three months after the apparent collapse of his supremacy, to produce the device now known as the quick-acting brake, which completely reversed the verdict just reached. Occasional hints would filter through the engineering press that there would soon be some important news to record, but not the most imaginative writer

would have ventured a guess at what actually happened; for, though the final product was still the
Westinghouse brake already known all over the
world, it had been reorganized by such changes as
reduced the time of the serial action of the brakes
on a fifty-car freight train to a little more than two
seconds, and enabled the locomotive driver to stop
the train, while speeding at forty miles an hour
down a steep grade, in less than half its own length,
not only without a sensible shock, but with not
even the slightest disturbance of the slideometer!

An illuminating incident occurred during this
last test at Burlington. The performance of electrically-operated brakes had been so brilliant that
the local atmosphere was highly charged with electric sentiment as related to the brake question. It
happened that, in the midst of the tests, one of
the business cars of the Burlington road, with several officers of the company aboard, anchored for
a night on the trial field. These gentlemen were,
of course, informed of the latest developments,
and when Westinghouse and some of his associates
made a social call on them, the conversation naturally
turned on the subject of greatest interest. Plainly
the visitors believed that the days of the automatic
air brake were numbered, and they expressed this
idea in sympathetic terms, doubtless with a view
of letting Westinghouse down gently. He, however, combated the notion that electricity, with
its uncertainty of action, could safely be depended
upon in a matter so vital as the braking of a train;
the results obtained in the tests, he admitted, were

interesting as experiments, but he regarded the devices used as impracticable in the then existing state of the braking and electrical arts. He was deep in this phase of the discussion when one of his hosts, thinking to order refreshments, pushed an electric button for the steward. There was no response, the bell refusing to ring. Instantly Westinghouse forced home his argument, declaring that the failure of the bell illustrated the untrustworthiness of electricity as a dependence in emergencies; if it could not be relied on to summon a waiter, how could we afford to confide to it the braking of a heavy train![1]

The confidence Westinghouse had expressed to his friend at the close of the public trials had not been mere vaunting; in the very hour when the shadows of defeat seemed closing in about him he had seen the point of weakness in his mechanism as it stood, and forecast a possible remedy. But in spite of all his knowledge and his faith, it was a

---

[1] As a matter of record it should be said that the brake which depended wholly upon electric operation of the air valves, after a splendid showing at Burlington, failed entirely in its last attempt to make a stop; the accident was due to the rupture of a conducting wire, and the train was brought to a standstill by gravity. The circumstances connected with the electrical phase of the Burlington trials well exemplified the foresight of Westinghouse in dealing with new problems. He was the original inventor of electro-pneumatic brakes, and presented at Burlington a simple method of providing electric actuation of the air valves; but, as we have seen, he perfectly realized the great practical difficulties which would be encountered in an attempt to use electricity as it would have to be employed in brake service, and felt sure that the electric art had not yet reached a stage of development which would justify its adoption for that purpose. He lived, however, to witness its successful application on subway trains in New York, Boston, and Philadelphia, the most critical and complex system of passenger transportation in the world.

giant's job to which he laid his hand. The cars on which the trials of 1886 and 1887 had been made were the property of his company; and he proceeded to arrange with the Chicago, Burlington, and Quincy Railroad management for the use of such locomotives and tracks as would enable him to experiment under the same conditions and on the same ground as those of the public trials. All the resources and all the employees available he kept at work day and night without cessation; the materials required from time to time, in every instance covering more than a carload, he ordered shipped from Pittsburgh to Burlington by express instead of freight, so that no time should be lost; and the experimental train of fifty cars had to be refitted, from stem to stern, not less than three times before he was satisfied with its work. But when, toward the close of September, the hindmost brake on the train clutched its wheel substantially the instant after the engineer's movement of his valve, his triumph made up for all the trouble he had undergone; for the last ground of criticism against the use of compressed air unaided by electricity in the operation of power brakes on long freight trains was disposed of.

Nor does the story end here. As the experiments outlined above had been wholly unofficial, and hence could not be formally authenticated by the committee of the Master Car Builders' Association, it was feared that inaccurate accounts might leak out and bias the judgment of interested parties. The Westinghouse Air Brake Company therefore decided to repeat the Burlington experiments in a number of important railroad centers like St. Paul, Chicago, St. Louis, Cincinnati, Cleveland, Buffalo, Albany, Boston, New York, Philadelphia, Washington, and Pittsburgh. To do this it was necessary to run the entire train of fifty cars from point to point, requiring two engines and in a few instances three, and involving operation under all the handicaps incidental to regular traffic. The fact that the train was nearly a half-mile long added to its difficulties, as it had to be conveyed over many roads the grades of which limited the length of trains to a much smaller number of cars.

One of the experiments which demonstrated the effectiveness of the latest improvements was dramatically interesting. With a fifty-car train at rest, observers were stationed at its rear end, and at a prearranged signal the engineer applied the brakes on the locomotive and blew the whistle at the same instant; and the sound of the whistle and the noise of the application of the brakes on the fiftieth car, about two thousand feet away, were practically simultaneous, showing that the transmission of power through the train was approximately at the speed of a sound wave.

Wherever a demonstration was made, invitations were extended to all local railroad men and others interested, and nearly every one was accepted. The final exhibition was at Pittsburgh in November, and was the concluding act in a development of the art of train braking carried on for a year at a total expense of probably not less than two hundred thousand dollars. The result obtained at so heavy a cost brought in immediately, however, large orders for the new brakes. The great trunk lines like the New York Central and Pennsylvania systems, adopting the quick-action brake as their standard, applied it not only to all the new cars they built, but also to their old cars that required general repairs.

The Master Car Builders' Association proceedings of 1888 included a report of its committee on freight-train brakes to this effect:

In our report to the Convention last year the main conclusion we arrived at was that the best type of brake for freight service was one operated by air, and in which the valves were actuated by electricity. Since that time your committee has not made any further trial of brakes, but the aspect of the question has been much changed by the remarkable results achieved in non-official trials which have taken place in various parts of the country, and have been witnessed by many of the members of this association. These trials show that there is now a brake on the market which can be relied on as efficient in any condition of freight service. The present position of the freight-train brake is briefly as follows:

"First. Brakes can be, practically speaking, simultaneously applied without electricity. throughout a train of fifty freight cars.

"Second. Other inventors are working at the problem of making an air brake which will be rapid in action and suitable for service on freight trains. We also understand that inventors are working at buffer and electric friction brakes, but we have no reason to hope that brakes upon these principles can successfully compete with air brakes."

In view of these conditions, your committee does not recommend the adoption of any particular brake, but considers that a freight train brake should fulfill the following conditions:

"First. It shall work with air of seventy pounds pressure. A reduction of eight pounds shall set the brakes lightly, and a restoration of pressure shall release the brakes.

"Second. It shall work without shock on a train of fifty cars.

"Third. It shall stop a train of fifty empty freight cars when running at twenty miles per hour within two hundred feet on a level.

"Fourth. When tried on a train of fifty cars it shall maintain an even speed of fifteen miles an hour down a grade of fifty-three feet per mile without variation of more than five miles per hour above or below that speed at any time during the descent.

"Fifth. The brakes shall be capable of being applied, released, and graduated on the whole train by the engineer, without any assistance from the brakemen or conductor.

"Sixth. The hose coupling shall couple with the present Westinghouse coupling."

That ended what has been picturesquely styled "the battle of the brakes," for, though it was literally true that the report contained the recommendation of no particular brake by name, its list of conditions which the ideal brake must meet could be fulfilled by no invention except Westinghouse's. The committee was discharged with the thanks of the Association after three years of arduous and painstaking investigation, of which by no means the least important outcome was an effective stirring of the public conscience on the subject of saving the lives and limbs of trainmen. Before the Burlington trials the subject of legislation making compulsory the use of power brakes on freight trains, though agitated by several benevolent persons and societies, had received but scant practical consideration, probably because it would have been futile to attempt to compel the use of a device not yet invented. Since the introduction of the quick-action brake, however, Congress has imposed the use of power brakes on all railways engaged in interstate commerce.

It must not be assumed that either his extraordinary activity in building up his air-brake industry in this country, or his frequent visits to Europe, had driven all other topics out of the mind of young Westinghouse. As early as 1875, during a stay in England, his curiosity was excited by some experiments in progress there with devices for railroad switching and signaling. It does not appear that at that time he undertook any improvements on the apparatus then under test; but his growing interest in the subject was preparing to bear practical fruit later, for we find him looking into the state of the art in the United States, and presently purchasing enough stock to give him control of the Interlocking Switch and Signal Company of Harrisburg, Pennsylvania, which owned a number of highly important patents on switching devices such as are used in steering a multitude of trains into and out of a great terminal station without confusion. His next move was to turn over his control of the company, together with a similar control he had acquired in the management of a Massachusetts company manufacturing electric signal apparatus, to a corporation styled the Union Switch and Signal Company, originally chartered in Connecticut but later in Pennsylvania. The Massachusetts member of the combination, it may be remarked in passing, was the first to employ the method of controlling signals by using the rails as electric conductors on the closed circuit principle — probably the most important single contribution to the art of signaling.

Meanwhile the busy mind of Westinghouse had been working out sundry details which took palpable form in a series of patents covering hydro-pneumatic and electro-pneumatic signaling — obviously the outgrowth of the familiarity gained with the properties and potentialities of compressed air during his long study of his braking problems. The first of these was issued on February 1, 1881, and between then and 1891 there were fifteen issues in his name.   He also was a liberal buyer of other men's patents which in his judgment possessed essential merit.   His first experimental mechanisms seem to have been hydro-pneumatic, but soon these were discarded in favor of electro-pneumatic devices, which have been tersely described by a distinguished engineer as "using compressed air for the heavy work, and electricity to pull the trigger."

A block system of safety signals was by no means a new idea at the time Westinghouse entered the field.   Leading railways had for many years been dividing their trackage into sections or blocks from a half-mile to four miles in length, and establishing at every junction of two blocks a signal station with a man in charge. This man would set a danger signal against coming trains until the man at the station next ahead telegraphed him that the track between them was clear of trains; then he would set an "all right" signal, and engineers were forbidden to pass from one block to another till this signal appeared. The arrangement was admirable as far as it went; but, as is always the case where mechanisms require human intelligence and muscular effort to manage them, it involved a margin of uncertainty. A watchman on night duty might drop asleep, or one on day duty might be suddenly overcome with illness, or any of a dozen conceivable mishaps might break the human link in the chain of operation and open the way for disaster. It was therefore deemed desirable to substitute automatic for human energy wherever practicable. In the electro-pneumatic system, as developed since Westinghouse entered the field, electricity has been made to do the watching and compressed air the signaling.

The chief and fundamental advantage of the automatic electric system over that into which a human agency must enter, is that, if a switch is turned or a rail broken, the continuity of the rails on that block, which carry the electric current that operates the signals, is broken, and the danger signal is set automatically. Many other ingenious devices have been put forth by this company, with the same electro-pneumatic coöperation for a basis, including one that automatically sets the brakes if a train passes a danger signal unheeded.

In the department of railroading we have just been considering, not less than in that to which he first addressed himself, the paramount object Westinghouse always held in view was to obtain the utmost utility in service compatible with the minimum peril to life and limb.

CHAPTER VIII

OPENING A MINE OF GASEOUS WEALTH

THE winter of 1883–1884 was passed by Mr. and Mrs. Westinghouse in New York City, where, early in the new year, a great happiness came to them with the birth of a son. It had been their desire to return to Pittsburgh as soon thereafter as would be prudent for mother and child, and with the coming of spring the family moved back.

In the home newspapers which had reached Mr. Westinghouse in New York had appeared so many references to the development of natural gas in Murrysville, a suburb of Pittsburgh, that his attention was strongly drawn to this subject. It had been known for all of fifty years that in various parts of Allegheny County, Pennsylvania, gas was to be had for the boring; still, no scientific estimates had been made of its abundance, and only a few manufacturers had seriously attempted to harness it for industrial purposes. As is so often the case with a product which has been evolved as one of the incidentals to a familiar operation, this gas was regarded as an interesting but not very valuable by-product of oil development, and those persons who did anything at all with it treated it more or less like a toy. But a balance had recently been struck in some experiments made at one large factory, the figures of which had caught the eye of Mr. Westinghouse and held it by their showing that in this plant the work performed by gas, besides being as satisfactory as that of any other fuel that had been tried, had effected a saving of a good many thousand dollars in a single year. If this were possible on a small scale, he asked himself, what might not be accomplished for the public profit and convenience if such a fuel could be made universally available?

As the train drew them nearer home, he opened the subject in conversation with his wife.

"You'd soon get as much absorbed in natural gas as you used to be in brakes when we first married," she answered in a jesting way; "but the brakes had one advantage over gas — you could always work out your problems at home, instead of running off to Murrysville every day."

"I can work out my problems at home just the same," he laughed in response; "that is, if you don't mind my boring a well through your flower beds. But don't charge me too much for the privilege. I dare say it will cost me five thousand dollars just to sink the hole and pipe it."

To the friends who heard gossipy echoes of this conversation, it seemed merely an exchange of harmless pleasantries; but those who passed the premises soon afterward realized that there had been something more than fun behind it. For there, not in the flower garden to be sure but back by the stable, stood the tangible evidences of an intention to probe the bowels of the earth, and a gang of men were already at work taking away the cut sod and stacking close at hand the necessary piping.

Day after day the chug-chug of the engine and the muffled stroke of the drill as it buried itself deeper and deeper in the earth kept the air in the neighborhood of the Westinghouse place vibrating, and furnished a text for a running fire of comment from the neighbors, some of it technically critical or inquisitive, some skeptical or semi-satirical. As a rule the people of Pittsburgh had already learned better than to question too boldly the probabilities of any large enterprise into which George Westinghouse went with a show of confidence, but a good many still were of open mind as to the practical value of such operations as he was conducting on his private grounds. An occasional glimpse could be caught of him at night, clad in overalls and standing near the men, watching every new development with the keenest concern; now giving an order, now consulting with the gang-boss, but never taking his eyes or his mind off whatever was in progress as long as he remained close at hand.

Nearly three weeks had been expended on the work, and a few of the ultra-wise heads had been shaken in doubt, when the foreman in charge one evening reported that he had detected traces of gas.

"How far down are you now?" asked Mr. Westinghouse.

"About 1560 feet."

"Are the signs of gas strong?"

"No, sir, weak; but I'm perfectly sure that a good supply is there, or not far away."

"The only way to find out is to go on. Perhaps by tomorrow we shall get results that amount to something. Only, go slow — feel your way along. Be very careful of the men, and warn them to take no risks."

That night Mr. Westinghouse went to bed late, fell into his usual sound sleep, and did not even dream of his gas well till, just before sunrise, he was roused with such suddenness that he sat bolt upright in an instant, wide-awake and staring around him. He was dimly conscious that what had startled him must have been an explosion of some sort; and — was that a continuing roar, or an echo from a former volume of sound which was still rumbling in his ears?

He was out of bed in a flash, and a few minutes later in the open air, not far from the spot where he had been talking with the foreman the night before. But what a change had come over the scene ! All about him and for many yards around, the lawn looked like a ragged seabeach after a storm. Gravel, sand, mud, dirty water, were everywhere, blanketing the once trim sward and well-kept paths under an indescribable mass of filth. The big, burly derrick that stood over the well opening had evidently received a severe blow, and a part of the pulley tackle at its top was gone. The drilling apparatus was nowhere to be seen at the moment, being ‘hidden beneath débris. The engine had been tossed aside like a squeezed orange, and lay some distance away, looking as if it had been rolled over and over in reaching its final resting place.

All these things he could make out only dimly. There was a hint in the east of the approaching dawn, and by holding his watch close to his eyes he could discern that it was about twenty minutes after three. Out of the mouth of the well a muddy geyser was still spouting into the air, with a loud noise that was between a hurricane roar and an angry volcanic rumble.

After the first effect of what he was witnessing had lost its vividness, he swept his surroundings with his glance, wondering at the absence of the men he had left there when he went to bed. A little later they emerged from the shadows one by one, like ghosts returning to a world from which they had been suddenly banished. Strangers came, too — persons who, within a mile radius, had been sleeping as calmly as he till roused by the explosion and set quaking with a nameless dread.

Item by item, in broken bits of explanation and conversation, the facts came out. Acting on his suggestion, the foreman had cautioned the workmen to proceed slowly and with care, and the drilling had gone on with such deliberateness that only a matter of fifteen feet had been accomplished before a savage growl issuing from the hole caused them to drop everything and run for their lives. They were not a minute too soon. Behind them as they fled for cover rose a great boom and roar, and then a shower of water, mud, and gravel which the light breeze spread about. Nobody had waited to see what more was coming, and the next thing they noted was the appearance of the master of the establishment on the scene.

The first expression of Mrs. Westinghouse as she looked out upon the spectacle of devastation a few minutes later was one of comic dismay. Her husband smiled inquiringly as her eyes met his.

"All things considered," said he, "are you satisfied with the experiment?"

"Oh, very well," she answered cheerfully. "The house still has a roof on it, and the kitchen isn't wrecked."

Breakfast was not much of a meal that morning · both husband and wife were too absorbed with the newest phenomenon.

The day was given up to devising ways and means for clearing away the rubbish. This had to be done at a disadvantage, because nobody about the premises, including the drill-gang, could feel positive as to what was coming next. The men had drilled a good many wells, first and last, but not one with the startling results of this performance.

Meanwhile the fountain of water and sand had subsided, and been succeeded by a stream of pure gas, which after a little lost its terrors as a novelty and provoked the spectators to various experiments. One man brought a chunk of coal weighing seven or eight pounds, and swinging it back and forth to get a tentative measure of distance, tossed it so that, if not intercepted, it would strike the exposed top of the piping. It went straight as directed, but, instead of alighting on the aperture, it was caught by the ascending jet of gas and lifted into the air like a chip in a gale, striking one of the beams of the derrick with great force and being smashed to pieces. Another adventurer, with the aid of a friend, dragged a heavy spruce plank to where they could push it crosswise over the opening. The stream of gas treated it as if it had been a strip of lath, breaking it in twain and entirely splintering a fragment that fell back so as partly to overhang the hole. Then somebody suggested that the derrick might be brought into play again to lower a big weight directly into the mouth of the well. A rope was attached to the upper rigging, and its loose end made fast to a stone that weighed perhaps a hundred pounds, and this was swung around so as to overhang the hole. The gas played with the intruder like a straw, shaking the weight free, and then lifting the loose rope into the air and holding it upright there, as straight and stiff as a flagstaff.

For nearly a week thereafter there was little sleep in the neighborhood, the well continuing to roar unceasingly night and day. But the resourceful mind of the inventor had been at work, and out of its cogitations emerged finally a stopcock which was a triumph of indirection in application and operation. By degrees the force of the flow was abated till it was shut off altogether, and the normal slumbers of the inhabitants of that part of the town were resumed not to be broken again for several nights. Then came some experiments in the evenings to test the illuminating quality of the gas. A pipe about sixty feet high had been built up from the mouth of the well, with a pulley fastened to its top, carrying a wire rope, the extremities of which dangled on the ground. To one of these extremities was attached a bundle of rags saturated with oil.

When all was ready, at a given signal the stopcock was turned so as to let the gas into the overhead pipe, and at the same time a match was applied to the rags and workmen began pulling on the free end of the rope. The burning torch ascended slowly till it reached almost the top of the rigging. Then a sudden strong pull finished its ascent, and a faint bluish flame was observed surrounding the rim of the pipe. The next instant, like a lightning flash connecting heaven and earth, a pillar of fire shot a hundred feet upward into the sky and was followed by a steady fountain of flame that was a marvelous study in colors. At its base was a jet of blue, brightening into pale yellow as it ascended, then becoming a dazzling white, and expanding like a tubular fan, the outer edges passing through various shades of yellow and orange into a sort of Indian red. The gas lamps of the city dwindled to little points of light, and persons in the street not less than a mile away were able to read distinctly the finest newspaper print by the light of the gigantic natural flambeau on the heights of "Solitude."

Unhappily the roaring noise which had so disturbed the repose of the neighbors at the outset was resumed while the gas was burning. It was not so bad as at first, but it was a serious enough nuisance to demand moderating. So, after the experiments had been repeated, with variations of detail, till the possibilities of the illuminant had been pretty well canvassed, the evening performances ceased, and Mr. Westinghouse announced that he was perfecting plans to connect his well with a system of city mains and dispense light and heat, and incidentally power, over a considerable area. The gas, he was satisfied, was of a quality markedly superior to anything produced by artificial processes, yet capable of being sold at a low price with a good profit. One of the large manufacturing concerns in Pittsburgh which was already using natural gas with fine effect was compelled to bring every foot of its supply from Murrysville, twenty miles away, at a cost of one hundred and twenty thousand dollars a year, and in a single ward a local company was collecting three hundred thousand dollars a year in gas bills. In yet other ways the Westinghouse discovery promised to work wonders for Pittsburgh; in none more potent than in changing a notoriously dirty city into a clean one.

But along with the bright prospects of the new enterprise came some decided drawbacks to be reckoned with. One of these was the exaggerated spontaneity of the supply, making it difficult to pinion it down to the work required of it. Gas artificially produced could of course be artificially regulated as well, but nature was a less compliant servant. The pressure she furnished was not measured by the immediate needs of the consumer or the peculiar exigencies of a situation: it came always and everywhere with unrestrained force, and the problem now before Westinghouse was how to make it obedient to the will of its employer. This demand was emphasized by the appearance in the newspapers, almost daily, of accounts of explosions or other accidents due to ill-regulated pressure, or popular ignorance of the best way of managing the unfamiliar fluid. Being invisible and almost odorless, it was always a menace, and its tremendous pressure forced it through every minute crevice, where, even if it were escaping from a carefully sunken main, it was liable to find its way through the softer spots in the soil. An accident resulting from this cause, which excited a great commotion in Pittsburgh and set everybody talking of the perils one must face in using natural gas, occurred in one of the large stables where a hostler struck a match one evening to light his lantern. A terrific explosion followed. The man was blown thirty feet through the air, a valuable horse was instantly killed, and the building was set afire and wrecked. It was then recalled that the stable stood on made ground; and as this was the case with most of the mills along the river front, there was, for a while, something like a suppressed panic in local manufacturing circles.

The underwriting companies, too, took a hand in the discussion, threatening to raise their rates to what would have been substantially prohibitory figures, unless changes were made in the method of transporting so dangerous an explosive. Some went

to the length of actually serving notice of the can-
cellation of certain outstanding contracts at a given
future date. The first thing Westinghouse did,
therefore, after arranging for the organization of
a company for the distribution and sale of the gas
from his well, was to invent a system of transportation. His initial improvement was to use two pipes,
one inside of the other. The inner pipe received
the gas from the original source, and carried it to
the entrances of the manufacturing establishments,
where its pressure remained nearly as at the well.
On the way, however, it was subject to constant
leakage, the pressure forcing infinitesimal jets through
the interstices in the joints of the pipe. But this
leakage, instead of passing into the earth, and so
on to cellars or other confined places where it was
dangerous, was caught in the outer pipe and then
permitted to escape to the atmosphere at a point
of safety. In later practice the joints of the conveying pipe only were inclosed with a protecting cover,
which was equivalent to the double pipe and greatly
reduced the cost as compared with using two complete lines of piping. Westinghouse also, in order
to reduce the cost of piping and dangers from undue
pressure, and make the ultimate product more
amenable to control for industrial purposes, arranged
a system of pipes of graded capacities, so that the
smallest took the gas directly from the well and the
larger ones allowed it an opportunity for expansion
till, by the time it was furnished to the consumer,
it was as easy to manage as gas produced from coal
by the ordinary process.

One of the details he had to work out gave West-inghouse a good deal of trouble, and not a few of his friends predicted that he would never be able to devise a satisfactory apparatus. Their skepticism merely stimulated him to fresh effort, which ulti-mately led to the production of a mechanism chiefly employed for domestic purposes and so arranged as to prevent a class of explosive accidents that had resulted in several fatalities.

For unavoidable reasons, the supply of gas was not infrequently interrupted without notice to users, and in such instances the fires would go out. When the gas was again turned on in the mains, if the outlets had not been closed, there would be an escape of gas which often, on account of its lack of odor, was not noticed until an attempt was made to re-light the fire. If there was an accumulation of gas, as was commonly the case, disastrous results would follow, and it became increasingly evident that some precaution was necessary, more effective than a mere admonition to the users to exercise great care. The problem was solved by the invention of a cut-off valve device, located in the supply pipe where gas was taken from the street mains into the building, and so organized that if, for any reason, gas was shut off from the mains, the valve automatically closed and could not be opened again until all the connec-tions in the building had been cut off.

The many advantages of gas for fuel purposes, as demonstrated on a vast scale in the natural gas development in Pittsburgh, at once awakened in the mind of Mr. Westinghouse great interest in the problem of the production of an artificial fuel gas that could be made available for localities removed from the natural gas fields. In coöperation with noted gas engineers he undertook a series of experiments extending over many years and involving large expenditures, hoping that a process for manufacturing gas might be developed that would make its general use for fuel purposes commercial. The net result of his investigations, though not materially advancing the art, led incidentally to the development of a producer for making gas from bituminous coal, that was a marked improvement upon similar devices then on the market. Its manufacture is still successfully continued.

CHAPTER IX

WHAT THE GAS DID FOR PITTSBURGH

THE difficulties of the situation were not confined to the solution of the problems already described. In order to carry gas from his well to the consumers, it was necessary for Westinghouse to obtain permission from the city authorities to lay pipes under the streets, and this meant tearing up pavements and more or less other disturbance of the routine of traffic. At once arose a commotion. Certain local dispensers of illuminating gas saw a peril to their business in the threatened invasion of the field by this "amateur", as they styled him, and their friends in the municipal Councils and on the press were encouraged to throw all sorts of obstacles into his way. He took pains at the outset to make it plain that he had no intention of asking a concession from the city without giving something in return, and his first application embraced an offer, if allowed to lay his pipes as indicated, to furnish the fire-engine houses and police stations with gas free of cost.

He was careful also to declare that he had no ambition to hold the sole control of the commodity, to make exorbitant profits, or to dictate arbitrary terms to any manufacturing interest, but would prefer a coöperative arrangement, whereby the business concerns that were likely to derive most advantage from the use of the gas should go in with him and share the advantages of his enterprise. "What I am seeking now," he said, "is to distribute the benefits of this discovery, receiving merely a fair compensation for my property — nothing more."

The first objection raised was that to grant to one person or company a privilege which was not thrown open on similar terms to whoever desired it would lead to all sorts of abuses, for the only way in which such a grant could be kept from putting the whole community under the yoke of a monopoly was to give to every applicant a permit to rip the highway to pieces, and for eminently practical reasons that seemed out of the question. A struggle of several weeks in the Councils ensued, the bone of contention being an ordinance so drawn, with the approval of Mr. Westinghouse, as to hinge his grant on the condition that he would undertake to convey the gas of any other producer through his pipes up to their capacity, the charge for such service to be arranged between him and his customers, and any disagreement referred to a trio of arbitrators. With every fresh outburst of opposition the reporters would run to him for an interview, evidently hoping to draw forth something in the way of a sensational denunciation; but he remained perfectly equable in mind and temper.

The old apprehensions excited by the explosive

quality of the gas were revived from time to time by some casualty, of which the hostile combination could always be trusted to make the most strenuous use.   One such occurred at "Solitude" which would have given his opponents a fine weapon if they had not fallen into the blunder of gross exaggeration in their first accounts of it and thus invited an anti-climax in its popular effect.   Two workmen employed to remove the outer pipe or casing at the mouth of the pioneer well and substitute another encountered a refractory joint, and ran a steel drill down beside it to loosen it.   As nearly as they could remember the details later, they kept the drill wet all the time; but the impact of the metals apparently produced a spark which ignited a jet of escaping gas, and in an instant they were in the midst of a sheet of flame and almost suffocated.   The blaze burned their eyes, faces, necks, shoulders and hands.   With a cry they staggered back and threw themselves into a bed of long grass, while other men working near by rushed to their assistance.   An alarm was sent to the nearest engine houses, and two hose companies were presently on the spot and playing streams upon the combustibles about the well, and, with the aid of a length of pipe and some wet blankets, the fire was suppressed.   The speed with which everything was done doubtless saved the day; but it did not prevent the wide circulation of a rumor that some laborers had been killed by gas on the Westinghouse place, and within an hour the yard was swarming with citizens and newspaper emissaries.   Instead of the tragedy for which they were looking, they found Mrs. Westinghouse taking care of two badly scorched workmen, for whom she had summoned her family physician. And thus an episode which the opposition at first counted upon to stir up public sentiment against further encouragement to the natural gas industry in Pittsburgh came to naught.

In due course, the Councils passed the desired ordinance, substantially as at first proposed. Meanwhile Mr. Westinghouse had organized a number of small companies, designed to divide between them the territory in which they should be the first comers in the field. There were not lacking, in the well on the "Solitude" estate, certain disquieting symptoms, which he interpreted to mean that he could not afford to rely upon that alone for his supply if he were going into the gas business on the scale he had in mind; so he drilled two or three more wells on his own premises and bought easements on many other pieces of property in the Murrysville district and elsewhere, and it was for handling these and making them tributary to the central concern that he organized his group of lesser companies.

But how was he to acquire the powers necessary to a corporation of the magnitude he wished to build up? It would have to procure rights of way by either purchase or condemnation before it could lay its pipes across private property anywhere. Besides that it must find, in Pittsburgh proper, some means of getting around an obstacle. The Fuel Gas Company, the head and soul of the opposition, had organized under an old law of Pennsyl-

"Solitude," the Westinghouse Home at Pittsburg

vania which conferred upon the public utility corporation of this character that was first to enter any given municipality a monopoly of its business there. Soon after the enactment of this statute there had been a tremendous activity in the creation of corporations, but a multitude of these mushroom affairs had since collapsed under the withering effect of a statute which conserved the life only of those that had been regularly organized to do business before its passage. John Dalzell, then engaged in the private practice of law in Pittsburgh and later a member of Congress, was Mr. Westinghouse's attorney, and to him Mr. Westinghouse turned in this emergency. Mr. Dalzell recalled the fact that several companies had taken out charters and gone into business under the old system, had bridged over the gap between the old and the new, and later had ceased to be active. As the capital of the State was the place where the records covering such matters were most likely to be available, he hastened to Harrisburg, where he laid the matter before an old professional friend who promptly announced: "I can put my hand upon the very thing you wish. Tom Scott procured from the legislature years ago a special charter for a corporation called the Philadelphia Company. He wanted it for the purpose of building a branch railroad tributary to the Pennsylvania system, but never used it, and in time it passed into other hands. This charter was so drawn that under it you can do almost anything you care to except engage in the business of banking. You can run a railroad, furnish a city with water, conduct a public cemetery, develop an oil-field —"

"Or produce and distribute natural gas?" suggested Dalzell.

"Surely."

"Then how does it come to be now on the market? Why isn't some one using it?"

"Well, that's hard to say. Whoever got hold of it finally proved a delinquent taxpayer, and the charter was sold under the hammer. I bid it in; and as the rights conveyed by it pass unimpaired to the purchaser at a tax sale, the charter is as good today as it was on the day the Governor signed it."

"How much can we get it for?"

"Thirty-five thousand dollars."

Dalzell whistled, but as his friend declined to consider any lower terms he carried the offer back to Pittsburgh with some misgivings. Mr. Westinghouse, instead of being irritated at the price named, received the news with apparent satisfaction, remarking:

"If the charter is all that is represented, I'll buy it. Go over it carefully and give me your written opinion."

Dalzell did so, reported in favor of the charter, and the money passed. Equipped now with all the weapons necessary for his fight with his confederated rivals, Westinghouse proceeded to launch the Philadelphia Company in its new domain.

Two special conditions contributed largely to hamper this undertaking. Not long before the company announced itself ready for business, the Penn Bank, a financial institution of supposed soundness

in which a great many Pittsburghers were deposi-
tors, had suddenly collapsed, and a series of mercantile failures occurred in and about the city. In
these circumstances, few people were favorably
inclined toward new and untested lines of investment. Then, also, a popular doubt had sprung
up, industriously cultivated by the hostile combination, as to how long the supply of natural gas would
continue sufficient in quantity to meet the extraordinary drafts which would be made upon it if all the
mills in the Pittsburgh district were to substitute
gas for coal. One statistician whose opinion was
generally regarded as reliable published an estimate
that the total consumption, including both manufacturing establishments and houses, but excluding
blast furnaces, would run as high as thirty million
feet a day. The local population, not accustomed
to figures of this magnitude, were taken by surprise,
and they had not yet fully recovered their breath
when Mr. Westinghouse, to whom the estimate
had been carried for criticism, met it, not with denials
or evasions, but with the still more startling declaration that the probabilities pointed to nearer four
hundred million feet. His own idea was that the
frankness of this announcement would tend to restore confidence rather than shake it further. He
discussed the matter on this basis with an old friend
whom he often consulted about financing problems,
and who presently inquired · "At what capitalization do you purpose starting your company?"

"In view of all the chances we must take," he
answered, "I don't believe we can afford to have

less than six million dollars to begin with. How does it look to you?"

"Your scheme is grand. If you had the wealth of the Indies to draw upon for making it go, you would rank with the world's great benefactors. But when you reflect that you have got to woo every one of those dollars from the purse of some one whose fright over recent events has made a dollar within reach look bigger than ten dollars he will have to wait for, you are tackling no light job."

"'Woo'? 'Fright'?" echoed Westinghouse. "Why, man, you don't know what you are talking about. There isn't a manufacturer in Pittsburgh so blind as not to be able to see what the future has in store for us here. When we announce that we are ready for subscriptions to our stock, there will be a rush for shares such as you have never seen or dreamed of. I shouldn't wonder if we had to engage a squad of police to keep order!"

In the Pittsburgh newspapers of August 4, 1884, appeared an advertisement filling between three and four columns, setting forth the prospectus of the Philadelphia Company, naming as its officers George Westinghouse, Junior, president, Robert Pitcairn, vice president, John Caldwell, secretary and treasurer. The board of directors included with these officers H. H. Westinghouse and John Dalzell. T. A. Gillespie also was mentioned as a stockholder, but with no office. The company, it appeared, owned all the gas rights on the "Solitude" property and sundry other tracts where it had already drilled wells or might thereafter drill them, as well as Westinghouse's patent Number 301,191, for a "system for conveying and utilizing gas under pressure", covering the features referred to in a previous chapter.

Possibly his consultation with his old friend was responsible for a slight change in the original plan, for we find that the capital stock of the company was fixed, for the time being, at only one hundred thousand dollars, although the advertisement announces an intention to increase this to five million dollars, "so that funds may be secured to operate largely in the distribution and supply of natural gas at whatever points, within the Commonwealth or without, there may be demand therefor." With the increase of capital, the gas wells and potentially productive territory controlled by Westinghouse, his patent on pipes for transporting gas, and the charter of the company, were to be put in at a valuation of two million, five hundred and fifty thousand dollars, the remainder of the five million dollars stock being offered to the public for subscription. This advertisement was repeated four times at later dates.

It is scarcely necessary to say that the expected rush did not materialize, and that the banks which had undertaken to receive subscriptions were able to go on with their ordinary routine of daily trade. After waiting long enough to satisfy himself that his fellow citizens generally did not share his glowing anticipations, Westinghouse made a canvass among his circle of personal friends, reënforcing the prospects held out in print with a running commentary of his own. As always happened at close contact, his enthusiasm proved infectious. In blocks ranging from a hundred shares to several thousand, he disposed of as much of the stock of the new corporation as was necessary to enable it to begin business, and before very long the rumors that it was turning out a money-maker caused a lively speculation in its shares. Its first dividends were at the rate of one per cent a month, but later it was thought prudent to reduce this to eight per cent a year. While Westinghouse was still its principal figure, his company put up a splendid office building in the heart of the business center of Pittsburgh, where, from the upper windows, he could look over at the strip of railroad track on which he made his first demonstration of the practical operation of his air brake.

In course of time, as some of the less hopeful prophets had predicted, the local use of natural gas for manufacturing was materially reduced. This was due partly to the diminished product of the near-by wells, which necessitated bringing in a supply from distant fields and at an increased cost, and partly to the comparative cheapness of the coal mined almost at the doors of the city, which experts have pronounced the finest manufacturing coal in the world. But natural gas is still used almost universally in Pittsburgh and its neighborhood for domestic purposes, and to a considerable extent in industrial lines.

While the direct results of the natural gas development in the Pittsburgh district were vast in their financial aspect, the indirect consequences are more difficult to comprehend or estimate. At about the time when the availability of gas for manufacturing purposes was demonstrated, the question of the best location for the economical production of iron and steel was receiving most serious consideration. Iron ores had theretofore been brought from the Northwest by lake and rail to Pittsburgh, because of the presence there of an ample and cheap supply of fuel necessary for the production of iron and steel. Some point on the shores of Lake Erie where the fuel and iron would meet, and thus save transshipment of the ore, appeared to offer inducements in the way of low production costs. The introduction of natural gas, however, for the time so changed conditions as to induce the establishment in the vicinity of Pittsburgh of many new large steel and iron industries that otherwise would probably have been located elsewhere. These have now become permanent, and, though the increased cost of natural gas has restored the fuel and iron ore situation to something like that which preceded the gas development, there is no reason to apprehend that the recognized availability of the Pittsburgh district for steel and iron manufacture will be disturbed.

Let it not be forgotten, either, that Pittsburgh learned for a while what it meant to be clean. During the natural gas régime, the pall of soot which had hung over the city for years, showering dirt on everything, was lifted, and many householders celebrated the relief by painting their dwellings white. The soot has now come back in sufficient quantity to be a nuisance, but ingenious minds are working on devices to get finally rid of it, as they would not have worked if the people had not enjoyed one refreshing draught of something better. Meanwhile the Philadelphia Company has expanded beyond recognition, adding one asset after another to its possessions, till today it controls substantially all the public utilities in the city and immediate suburbs.

CHAPTER X

The Contest of the Currents

THE Westinghouse Machine Company was organized in 1880, originally to build high-speed engines of a type invented by Herman Westinghouse. A contract having been made with the Brush Electric Company to furnish it with these engines for use with direct-driven dynamos in its system of arc lighting, Herman had occasion to make a night trip from New York to Boston, and in the smoking room of his sleeper fell into conversation about his errand with a young man who dropped the remark that he, too, was interested in electric illumination, but in a more immediate way, having recently invented a self-regulating dynamo which he believed would solve one of the most vexatious problems in incandescent lighting. Up to that time the dynamos made by the Edison Company, the leading concern in the incandescent field, had required regulation by hand in order to keep the current suitably proportioned to the drafts made upon it; without this, the extinction of one lamp would throw an additional force into all the others drawing upon the same source of supply, with a consequent waste of both current and material. The self-regulating dynamo, of course, eliminated the expense and uncertainty of the human factor. The inventor invited his new acquaintance to call on his return, and look at the machine, introducing himself as William Stanley, an electrical engineer by profession.

Although nothing of importance resulted immediately from this meeting, it paved the way for relations of much intimacy in later years, when George Westinghouse, having become interested in what he learned about the dynamo and about a lamp of Stanley's invention, engaged the young man to conduct sundry experiments in the same line at the works of the Union Switch and Signal Company, and out of these grew the first electrical apparatus manufactured under the Westinghouse auspices. The enterprise was not extensive in its beginnings, consisting chiefly of supplying apparatus for incandescent lighting in competition with the Edison Company, there being little difference between the two systems except for the important self-regulating feature of the dynamo. One of its indirect effects, however, was to bring sharply to the attention of Westinghouse the limitations of the direct current system then exclusively employed for lighting and power purposes, ultimately leading to his early identification of the great advantage to be derived by the substitution of the alternating system for the direct system. And thus we approach the verge of one of the hardest fought wars that ever occurred in the scientific field, the contest of the currents.

For the reader's better understanding, it may be said that a direct or continuous current is comparable to water made to flow through a pipe always in one direction, whereas an alternating current is as if the same water were made to flow through the pipe first in one direction and then in the other, the reversals of direction occurring a great many times in a single second — an expedition which would be possible only in so imponderable an essence as electricity. The result to the user of electricity is practically the same with either system, except in the matter of cost. With the direct system it is necessary to generate and distribute the current at a pressure, or voltage, that will not burn out the filament of incandescent lamps. As this pressure is relatively very low, and the quantity of electricity that can be conveyed by wires is dependent upon the pressure at which it is being distributed, the cost of the conducting wires, constituting a large part of the investment in an electric production and distribution system, is greatly increased as compared with the alternating system; in the latter, very high electrical pressures can be employed, with a proportionate reduction in the cost of the distributing wires, and then, by simple and cheap mechanisms, transformed or converted to the required low pressures at the point of use

At the time we are now considering, the popular impression was general that it would be out of the question to employ the alternating current for incandescent lighting, inasmuch as such high pressures would burn out the filaments of incandescent lamps. Moreover, there prevailed a widespread terror of an invisible agent with such a capacity for the destruction of life by shock and of property by fire. To the discovery of some means whereby the mighty resources of the alternating current could be placed, with reasonable safety and for a price not prohibitive, at the disposal of whoever wished to use it for impelling the machinery of manufacture, for lighting streets, halls and houses, or for easing the difficulties of housekeeping, Mr. Westinghouse directed his own ingenuity and devoted that of the little scientific corps he gradually gathered about him.

During one of her journeys abroad, Mrs. Westinghouse had fallen dangerously ill and been restored to health by the skill of an Italian physician named Pantaleoni. Mr. Westinghouse was deeply grateful, and, when he found that Guido Pantáleoni, the doctor's son, had inherited a scientific bent, he brought the young man to this country and gave him a responsible position in the employ of the Union Switch and Signal Company. Albert Schmid, a Swiss engineer of great competence, whom Mr. Westinghouse had met while looking into certain arc-light experiments in Paris, came over about the same time and was taken on, his special function being to design and construct the dynamos needed to carry into practical effect the discoveries reported by Stanley from the laboratory. Member after member was thus added to the staff, which later included, as the chief's interest in electrical matters grew more intense, Oliver B. Shallenberger, Nikola

MARGUERITE ERSKINE WESTINGHOUSE

Tesla, Reginald Belfield, Charles F. Scott, Lewis B. Stillwell, Loyall A. Osborne, and several other gifted and ambitious young engineers who have since become famous in their own right.

The fundamental limitations of the direct current system, already pointed out, had been fully developed during the early '80s, and the exorbitant cost of distribution, due to the heavy copper wire necessary to be used, threatened to be still further enhanced by an increase in the cost of copper. When to this was added the multiplication of distributing stations necessitated by the short carrying distance of the direct current, Westinghouse felt that hard and fast bounds had been set to the expansion of the industry. The London technical weekly, *Engineering*, had paid unusual attention, as early as 1883, to certain letters patent issued jointly in Great Britain to a brace of collaborators, a French electrician named Lucien Gaulard and an English engineer named John Dixon Gibbs. Their invention consisted of a system for distributing alternating currents through "transformers", and their mechanism had made its first public appearance at an electrical show held in the Westminster Aquarium.

The earlier printed references to the device seem not to have particularly appealed to Westinghouse; but in the spring of 1885 he became very much interested in some descriptive and illustrated articles dealing with the electric lighting department of an International Inventions Exhibition just opened in South Kensington. On this occasion lamps manufactured by his own company were among

the foreign products displayed. A competing concern was showing a number of its lamps of different
types, every one fed by a current obtained from a
Gaulard-Gibbs "secondary generator", which, as
Engineering explained, was an apparatus designed
to make it possible to carry a large amount of electrical energy on a small conductor, and draw it off
at various points in such quantities and under such
pressure conditions as might be required. From a
single small main were fed large and small arc lamps,
Jablochkoff candles and incandescent lamps, requiring varying electromotive forces. At every
place where there was a lamp or group of lamps of
one character, a secondary generator or transformer
was inserted into the circuit, and a part of the
energy flowing in the main and primary circuit
was made to induce a corresponding and nearly
equal amount of energy in a local secondary circuit,
of the required electrical pressure.

On the strength of this testimony, Westinghouse
arranged to import a few of the Gaulard-Gibbs
transformers. They arrived in the autumn of 1885,
and the tests to which they were subjected by Mr.
Westinghouse's electricians of the Union Switch
and Signal Company during the next few months
satisfied him that the European inventors had hit
upon one idea for which he had long been searching ;
for his success in sending natural gas through relatively small pipes and high pressure over long
distances, and distributing it to consumers under
reduced pressure, led him to believe that electric
current could in the same way be advantageously

distributed at high voltage and locally reduced by transformers, or converters, as they then were called. Mr. Stanley, with the assistance of some of his junior colleagues, conducted a series of experiments which showed that the serial system of Gaulard and Gibbs should be changed to a multiple-arc, or parallel, arrangement of transformers. The difference may be illustrated in miniature by supposing a current to be arranged to feed ten lamps, set serially in a circle, by passing from lamp to lamp over an intervening wire; now, if anything happens to one of the lamps and interrupts the current there, all the lamps must go unfed; whereas, if the same ten lamps were separately supplied, each having its individual wire to it from a common main, any one could be cut off without stopping the flow to the rest. This last condition illustrates roughly the multiple-arc or parallel system, as distinguished from the serial.

It was soon found that the ratio of transformation of which the Gaulard-Gibbs converters were capable was insufficient for the purposes the Company had in view, and special transformers, therefore, had to be designed. Westinghouse arranged with Stanley, whose health had become impaired, to go to Great Barrington, Massachusetts, and establish an experimental laboratory for the development of better types of generators and transformers. Here Stanley constructed about a dozen transformers designed to reduce a five-hundred-volt main line potential to one hundred volts in the secondary, and, in the spring of 1886, placed these in successful operation and lighted several stores in the village. This was the first installation of the transformer system in this country to furnish outside lighting.

Meanwhile, one afternoon in February, in the first flush of satisfaction over some very recent accomplishment, Mr. Westinghouse had telegraphed Franklin L. Pope, his New York patent lawyer and an expert in electrical science, to take the next day's steamer for England. Pantaleoni, who was in Pittsburgh at the time, was dispatched by the first train to New York to join Pope and accompany him abroad. The interview at which he received his instructions was short and to the point. The explanation of the errand on which Pope and he were about to start was condensed by Westinghouse into a simple command to find Gaulard and Gibbs and buy their patent rights for the United States, and all the young man ventured to inquire was: "How much are we to pay for the rights?"

"They'll tell you their price," was the terse response. "Whatever it is, close the bargain, and I'll send the money by cable to you."

Within a month the two men were back in this country, bearing the assignment of the patent rights desired, for which they had paid fifty thousand dollars. Westinghouse had some difficulty at first in getting his acquired rights recognized by our Patent Office, but by September this tangle was cut. His staff, who in the interval had been studying the possibilities of this latest system of distribution, now attacked their task afresh from their better vantage ground.

A convenient opportunity having arisen for removing the works of the Union Switch and Signal Company to the suburb of Swissvale, its old quarters in Garrison Alley, Pittsburgh, were fitted up as a factory for making electrical apparatus, and a corporation organized under the title of the Westinghouse Electric Company took over this branch of the Union Switch and Signal Company's business. Here was constructed a new alternating-current constant-potential dynamo invented and designed by Stanley. By the following autumn the Electric Company was prepared to make an impressive demonstration. A number of converters and four hundred lamps were placed in a building at Lawrenceville, about four miles from the dynamo which was operated at first to supply one thousand volts and afterward two thousand. The lamps fed from this current were kept burning continuously for a fortnight. Westinghouse visited them daily to observe their action. It was the first successful exhibition ever made in the United States of the transmission of electrical energy for any considerable distance through the medium of the alternating current. The same dynamo, with converters, was then removed to Buffalo, New York, and placed in actual service on the night before Thanksgiving, 1886.

The tests having gone far enough to leave no room for doubt of what could be accomplished, orders began to come in for the new apparatus, which promised to revolutionize electric lighting by so reducing the necessary cost as to put small towns substantially on an equal footing with large ones as to public illumination. Greensburg, about twenty miles from Pittsburgh, is credited with having been the first town to procure a complete municipal plant using the Westinghouse alternating current system. The business of the Company advanced at a rate with which it was almost impossible to keep apace in manufacturing; the works had to be enlarged, and within two years the force employed there numbered three thousand men.

Not every obstacle, however, had yet been cleared from the path of the new company. Of two things it stood sorely in need: a meter which would accurately gauge the amount of electrical energy dispensed or applied, and a power motor. Both came soon. In the spring of 1888, Shallenberger was examining an arc lamp to which Lange, another of Westinghouse's engineers, had invited his attention, when a small spiral spring chanced to drop out of place and lodge upon the top of the magnet spool near the projecting core. The friend was about to pick it up, when Shallenberger caught his arm, saying quickly: "Wait! Let's see what makes that spring revolve." The spring, which was about an inch in length and of the diameter of a lead pencil, was slowly rotating on its longitudinal axis. They watched it silently for a while, when Shallenberger exclaimed: "I will make a meter out of that!" Precisely four weeks from that day he had a completely developed alternating-current meter to exhibit to his colleagues, and by August it was ready to place on the market.

It was to Tesla — described by one of his associates of those days as "an inspired genius, into whose mind inventions sprang as the conception of a great picture projects itself upon the imagination of an artist" — that the Company owed its desired motor. By an odd coincidence, on the day following the incident with the meter, Ferrari published in Italy a description of an electric motor operating on essentially the same principle as the Shallenberger meter; and about four weeks later Tesla's description of his own motor was presented to the American Institute of Electrical Engineers in New York. Tesla and Ferrari, separated by three thousand miles, had independently of each other, but simultaneously, worked out the theory on which the modern alternating-current motor operates. Tesla was the earlier accredited inventor of the motor itself, having filed his applications for patents a considerable time before the Ferrari publication, and his discoveries went further than Ferrari's, including a polyphase system which was more satisfactorily adapted to the distribution of large power units.

It must not be supposed that all the more recent activity of the Westinghouse Electric Company had escaped the notice of the concerns engaged in the manufacture of direct current electrical apparatus. They had at first treated it as a passing phase of business rivalry, but, with the developments just mentioned, they awoke to a realization that a field which they had had for so long practically to themselves had been invaded by a rival too powerful to resist with merely defensive tactics.

The aggressive warfare which was opened forthwith upon George Westinghouse and his industry can be fully appreciated only by reading the newspapers of that day. Advertising columns, news columns, and editorial columns were employed indiscriminately to carry on the campaign, of which anything like a full history would require several volumes as large as this. The summary that follows, however, will suffice to indicate its scope and spirit.

CHAPTER XI

THE STRUGGLE IN NEW YORK

IN pursuance of his custom of carrying his goods to the largest market, Westinghouse took speedy steps to introduce his lighting system into New York city in competition with the systems already on the spot. That was before the era of underground telegraphy, and the streets had for years been disfigured with the unsightly poles laden with telegraph and telephone wires; so that, when electric illumination began its career there, such additional wires as it required were, as a matter of course, strung in like manner.

Although arc lights, fed by high potential direct currents, had been obtrusively in evidence everywhere in New York since the early '80s, their feeding mains appear to have aroused little criticism as a nuisance; but with the advent of the Westinghouse enterprise, all overhead cables suddenly leaped into prominence not only as eyesores but as a public peril. Leading newspapers which till then had confined their discussion to the expediency of exchanging gas for electricity, began, with astonishing unanimity, to make a display of every happening that could be used to excite animosity in the popular mind toward the alternating current. A boy peddler was killed by contact with a wire that hung too low; a repairer was stricken while mending an insulator at the top of a pole: at once the incidents were seized upon and the most was made of them for their local effect, regardless of how much or how little the character of the current had to do with the matter. When a horse stepped upon a fallen wire in Buffalo and it and its driver were killed, or a wooden house in Pittsburgh was set ablaze by contact with an exposed conductor, despatches descriptive of the painful details, often rendered more lurid by the imaginative narrator, were promptly telegraphed to New York. A few dailies set up a special department for injuries inflicted, damage suits entered, charitable funds started for adults crippled or children orphaned — all in consequence of the indifference of the great mass of the citizens to the arch destroyer hovering over their heads! One fatal accident was exploited through ten papers of the following day, in articles from a half-column to five columns long, under this variety of headings in exaggerated type:

Horrible Death of a Lineman.
The Wire's Fatal Grasp.
One Martyr More.
Wire Has Another Victim.
The Electric Murderer.
Another Lineman Roasted to Death.
Electric Wire Slaughter.
Again a Corpse in the Wires.
Death's Riot.
Electric Wires Add to Their List of Victims.

Abram S. Hewitt, Mayor of the city, was frantically besought to take the law into his own hands, if need be, and strip the wires from their places; and a particularly strenuous journal carried its denunciation of his inaction so far as to propose that he be arrested and locked up or fined as accessory to "a carnival of avoidable homicide." This line of agitation at first appeared to come almost wholly from inexpert or at least nonprofessional sources; but presently arose one Harold P. Brown, an electrician by calling, who, not content with denouncing the survival of overhead wires in a great city, made the alternating current itself, wherever found or however used as a public utility, an object of attack. He obtained the use one day of a lecture room at the Columbia School of Mines, and issued invitations to a demonstration he was about to make of the difference between the death-dealing alternating current and the comparatively harmless continuous current. He had in his audience representatives of the municipal Board of Electrical Control, several members of the Electrical Institute, and a goodly group of reporters for the press. After putting a big black dog to torture with applications of an alternate current at various pressures, he dispatched the poor creature with a heavier shock, and was about to produce a fresh victim when the superintendent of the Society for the Prevention of Cruelty to Animals interfered.

"You've demonstrated how many volts will kill a man," he exclaimed, "and that's enough. The show can't go on!"

Brown protested, but to no avail; so he left the

audience to muse on his statement that in former tests, though he had applied a continuous current of more than fourteen hundred volts to a dog without producing death, he had repeatedly killed dogs with from five to eight hundred volts of an alternating current. The performance was most cleverly staged, and for the ends Brown had in view its sudden interruption by a benevolent agent only heightened its spectacular effect. The sole suggestion of an anticlimax came when he issued a challenge to the unbelieving.

"I am aware," said he, "that certain defenders of the alternating current declare that they have received a thousand volts without injury. Would any one present like to take a thousand volts?"

One skeptic promptly responded that he had a friend there — an electrical expert — whom he would put forward to take a thousand volts of alternating current, if Brown would prove his faith by taking a thousand volts of continuous current. Brown declined on the ground that the proposal was foolish; and, as the friend who had been offered for sacrifice on the altar of science seemed relieved at this retort, the discussion ended and the gathering dispersed, but not until Brown had oratorically declared that the only places where the alternating current ought to be permitted were " the dog pound, the slaughter house, and the State prison." This last suggestion derived a timely significance from the fact that the New York legislature had, but a few weeks before, amended the criminal code by the substitution of electricity for hanging as the death penalty, and

Mr. Brown had been one of the authorities most depended on by the special advocates of the change.

Mr. Westinghouse and his friends took pains to make plain that they would welcome any practical plan for taking all wires out of the air and running them underground.   The demands made upon Mayor Hewitt were met with the calm response that he would be most happy to remove all obstructions from the highways as soon as he could see his way clear to do so without producing more bad than good results; and that, instead of trying to drive any particular electric system out of business, the more sensible course would be to retain the benefits of all for the public but subject their traffic to careful regulation.   Still there was no silencing the complainants, whose continued assaults gradually wore upon the nerves of their adversaries.   The atmosphere became, for a while, thick with the personalities, including charges of interested motives and even of bribery and fraud, volleyed back and forth between the champions of the respective systems.   Nobody was spared.   A letter written by ex-Governor Cornell to the Mayor, urging the absolute prohibition of high-tension circuits anywhere within the city limits, came in for some sarcastic comments at a convention of the National Electric Light Association held in New York late in the summer of 1888.

Doctor P. H. Van der Weyde read a paper on the "Comparative Danger of the Alternating vs. Direct Currents" in which he declared that Brown's assumptions on this head were erroneous because the criterion on which he based his comparison was scientifically defective, and added that, while danger lurked in both, it was no greater in the alternating than in the continuous system. The convention attested its sympathy with this view by unanimously adopting, amid great applause, a series of resolutions condemning "the persistent efforts of rival interests to educate the public to a distrust of high-potential electric currents", as liable to instigate unfair legislation, and declaring it "entirely possible to produce and distribute high-tension currents for public use without any more danger or difficulty than attends the distribution of gas and water in our dwellings."

This unqualified assurance from an organization representing the highest electrical talent in America did not have its hoped-for effect upon the press, which, though quoting it with every mark of respect for the Association, continued to berate the alternating current and its promoters. One newspaper created a sensation in the slum districts, where pictures appealed much more to the popular emotions than any kind of reading matter, by spreading on its first page a hideous cartoon showing a graveyard, with headstones bearing the names of the victims of the wires who had already been buried, and an open grave, with a coffin beside it, waiting for the next on the list. Interviewers pursued Westinghouse wherever he went, trying to lure him into some explosive utterance against Thomas A. Edison, the chief exponent of the continuous current, which might produce a personal collision between the two inventors, and thus set free a fund of spicy "copy." But on the one or two occasions when he did consent to speak, nothing more violent than this was forthcoming:

"The alternating current will kill people, of course. So will gunpowder, and dynamite, and whisky, and lots of other things; but we have a system whereby the deadly electricity of the alternating current can do no harm unless a man is fool enough to swallow a whole dynamo."

And in a letter to one paper which, though critical, had seemed inclined to be fair, he wrote:

"The alternating current is less dangerous to life from the fact that the momentary reversal of direction prevents decomposition of tissues, and injury can result only from the general effect of the shock; whereas in a continuous current there is not only the injury from the latter cause, but a positive organic change from chemical decomposition, much more rapid and injurious in its effects. A large number of persons can be produced who have received a one-thousand volt shock from alternating currents without injury, and among them a wireman who became insensible and held his hand in contact with the wires for a period of three minutes without fatal results — in fact, was able to go on with his work after a short period.

"The alternating system not only permits the use of a current of one thousand volts for street mains, but requires its conversion into currents of fifty volts or less for house-wiring. The converters are so constructed that the primary or street current can never by any possibility enter the house. . . . No person coming in contact with the alternating current as used for domestic lighting would be aware of its presence."

Even the most sober of the great periodicals were drawn into the controversy. An article on "The Dangers of Electric Lighting", arraigning the alternating current, by Thomas A. Edison, appeared in the *North American Review*, and "A Reply to Mr. Edison", by George Westinghouse, in the next month's number.

It was characteristic of the temper and methods of the forces arrayed against him that no sooner were they convinced that Westinghouse was sincere in his desire for some practical plan for sinking the wires underground than they began to cry out that, though telephone and telegraph and other direct-current wires might be placed there with safety, the alternating-current wires could not. A start had been made upon a scheme of electric-wire subways, but the contractors who had it in charge were so slow that the work came presently to what amounted to a dead standstill. In the midst of the turmoil Hugh J. Grant succeeded to the mayoralty, and his office became the storm-center of a tremendous struggle which lasted about two years, and was punctuated at intervals by court orders, injunctions, and counter-injunctions, and by raids made upon the overhead wires by gangs of municipal employees under orders to cut away all that were improperly insulated, obstructively hung, or otherwise liable to be dangerous.

Many of the laborers employed in these forays, not being trained for their task, made costly mistakes of indiscrimination, cutting inoffensive wires and severing important connections. As a result, the great city was left almost in darkness at times, as arrangements for going back to lighting the streets with gas were not easily perfected. But finally peace was restored on a basis which, if not to the entire satisfaction of all parties, at least permitted the subway system to be finished and the overhead wires transferred to it; and, but for an occasional quarrel over rental privileges or the like, New York resumed its normal night illumination, and something like order settled down where chaos had reigned before.

In view of the generally efficient electric service enjoyed by all cities now, and the enormous extent to which the alternating current has come to be used for lighting, cooking, running machinery large and small, and after-dark advertising, with comparative freedom from casualties, it is amusing to recall the dismal warnings put forth by as brilliant a man as Mr. Edison a generation ago. He was freely quoted in newspaper interviews as positive that no known method of insulation could render a high-tension alternating wire safe; and that, as for subways, they would not lessen the danger, because the high-tension current would burn out the tubes and enter dwellings through the manholes. He insisted that if the alternating current were to be used at all in New York, its maximum pressure must be reduced to two hundred volts. Some of his more radical disciples went so far as to argue that to take the obnoxious wires out of the upper air and run them through subways would only multiply the perils with which they menaced life and property. •

All this is, of course, so old a story now that we can afford to laugh over it without wasting further space on a rehearsal of details. One incident of the fight upon the alternating current, however, to which I have made but a casual allusion before, was too theatrical in character to be passed thus summarily. I refer to the adoption by the State of New York of what is commonly styled electrocution.

The sensibilities of all humane people had been shocked so often by ill-managed hangings, that on Governor Hill's recommendation the Legislature of 1886 created by statute a commission composed of three citizens conspicuous for their intelligence, philanthropy, and high character, to consider the question of a change in the method of executing the death penalty. These gentlemen spent more than a year on their inquiry, and then Elbridge T. Gerry, their chairman, presented a report in favor of using the alternating electric current, and an act to that effect was passed; but coupled with the main provision were several others regarding the mode of confinement of the condemned person, his privileges in the death-ward, the discretionary hour of the execution, the functionaries who must witness it, and the silence which must be maintained by the press as to everything except the bare fact that such an event had occurred.

At once arose a chorus of belated protests from persons who had ignored their opportunity to present their objections to the Commission or the Legislature.

Some criminal lawyers denounced the proposed punishment as "cruel" and "unusual" within the intent of the Constitutional prohibition; a physician here and there voiced his judgment that the electric current shot through a human being would torture him fearfully before killing, and that at best its mortal effectiveness was open to question; scores of sentimentalists censured the preliminary precautions and the provisions as to witnesses; and most of the newspapers which had been accustomed to print long and elaborate accounts of hangings fell afoul of the restrictions on publicity. This promiscuous agitation prepared the popular mind for what was coming next — the announcement that Harold P. Brown had obtained a contract for furnishing the apparatus needed for disposing of the first malefactor doomed to suffer death under the new law. He was one William Kemmler, an ignorant and besotted creature, more brute than man, who, in a fit of anger, had hacked a dissolute woman to death with an ax. All the circumstances of the murder were so revolting that whatever was associated with it in any way seemed to suffer a taint from the contact, not excepting the instrument of death with which society proposed to avenge the crime. And then the further news came out that Mr. Brown had equipped not only the Auburn State prison, where Kemmler had been condemned to die, but Sing Sing and Clinton as well, with complete Westinghouse outfits, one of which, he said, had "already a record as a man-killer"; and that, apparently in order to escape the danger of a refusal if he tried to make his purchase direct, he had bought his apparatus of middlemen. The indignation of Westinghouse passed all bounds, but he kept its outward expression under strong control, and, beyond a fresh refutation of the slurs cast at his system by falsehoods or half-truths, held his peace for a time to await events.

Immediately after his sentence, Kemmler's attorneys began a series of appeals which for industry and ingenuity have never been surpassed in their way. The challenge to the constitutionality of the new law was threshed out so completely that not a shred of doubt remained; a canvass of the scientific question also was carried as far as the endurance of the courts could be stretched, and included a hearing before a referee, at which Edison and Brown were the star witnesses called to prove the deadliness of the alternating current. The battle for Kemmler's rescue even invaded the Legislature, where Newton M. Curtis, for half a lifetime a propagandist against judicial homicide, succeeded in pushing through the Assembly a bill to abolish capital punishment altogether in New York, but, the Senate refusing compliance, his efforts came to naught.

As Kemmler was penniless, and the customary fees of lawyers like William Bourke Cockran and Roger M. Sherman were far from trifling, a suspicion gained place in the public mind for a season that Westinghouse stood with his purse behind these strenuous attempts to stay the hand of justice, in the hope of saving the offspring of his faith and courage from being "turned to hangman's uses." There was never a shadow of evidence forthcoming, however, to justify such an inference; and when Westinghouse himself condescended to deny the rumor, that ended the matter. Every defensive resource, State or Federal, having been exhausted, sentence was pronounced for the third and last time, and on August 6, 1890, Kemmler was put to death in the electric chair.

In his official report on the execution, Doctor Carlos F. MacDonald, the supervising physician, made the unqualified assertion that, in comparison with hanging, "electricity is infinitely preferable, both as regards the suddenness with which death is effected, and the expedition with which all the preliminary details may be arranged. . . . In other words, it is the surest, quickest, and least painful method that has yet been devised." Such a verdict from such a source lulled the tumult except among a few representatives of the yellow press; and, as soon as the sensational features of the case lost their popular appeal, nearly everybody passed from considering arguments against tolerating the employment of the alternating current for public utilities, to searching for new lines of industrial production or social convenience to which it could be applied.

CHAPTER XII

ORIGIN OF THE "STOPPER" LAMP

THE reader can hardly have failed to discover that the fertility of mind and the self-confidence which distinguished George Westinghouse were combined with a charm of personality that attracted men to him on short acquaintance, and a masterful quality to which they responded almost unconsciously with compliance. These traits made him not only the titular head of any enterprise he started, but substantially a dictator in its management. As nearly everything industrial to which he laid his hand involved a large initial outlay, he made a practice of organizing corporations in which, while the stockholders furnished the necessary funds for launching them and elected their boards of directors, he was before long the supreme figure. This system had its marked advantages as far as simplicity and ease of administration were concerned; it had some equally marked drawbacks. Human nature is so constituted that the man who has succeeded in all his first endeavors is liable to acquire the notion that he is invincible, and to be led into ventures beyond his strength.

Such was the case with Westinghouse. By the spring of 1890 he was in control of concerns which were manufacturing air brakes and switch and signal apparatus for steam railroads; making pioneer experiments with electric railways for local traffic; furnishing natural gas to a large district tributary to Pittsburgh; running small industrial plants that could utilize the gas effectively; turning out every kind of mechanism for the generation and distribution of the alternating electric current; and furnishing electric illumination to communities in all the American States and Territories and in various other parts of both hemispheres, even the Chinese city of Canton having contracted for an equipment. In four years the total annual sales of the appliances produced by his Electric Company had grown from one hundred and fifty thousand to four million dollars.

Although the unwholesome trade situation which was developing in the country at large had not yet reached its crucial stage, it was already threatening enough to cause uneasiness in many minds. In the midst of a violent agitation of the silver question in the United States, news suddenly came from England of the collapse of the great banking house of the Baring Brothers, carrying down a bevy of lesser concerns and spreading everywhere a fear of worse things still to come. Mr. Westinghouse, who had run up to Lenox, Massachusetts, to attend to a real estate purchase there, was summoned back to Pittsburgh by telegraph. He realized at once that the Electric Company was facing a crisis. His first act was to call together the directors and lay before them a scheme of relief which involved, as a preliminary feature, the change of the title of their corporation to the Westinghouse Electric and Manufacturing Company, and the doubling of its capital stock. The old shareholders were given the privilege of subscribing to the stock at a price twenty per cent below par, but general commercial conditions were so depressing that the response fell far short of what he had hoped. He thereupon invited the leading bankers of Pittsburgh, who had profited by the business brought them through the industries he had built up in the city or had attracted thither from the outside, to meet him for an informal talk. A good many came; but several on whom he had most surely counted failed him — one going so far as to confess to a friend that he dared not expose himself to the persuasive influence of Westinghouse face to face, for fear of yielding to impulse and granting a loan which he would afterward regret.

The meeting opened with a brief review by Westinghouse of his connection with local institutions, laying special stress on the growth of his Electric Company, which, in spite of its temporary embarrassment, was destined for a career of unparalleled prosperity. Then he set the sum he must have at once at a half-million dollars, offering collateral security for such an accommodation, including a mortgage on his estate at Homewood, which had largely increased in value since its purchase nearly twenty years before. So favorable an impression did he create that the bankers appointed a committee to go over the whole subject and report at an adjourned meeting. The report was favorable, and in a short time the half-million desired was oversubscribed.

But just at this point one of the subscribers suggested that, if they were going to pull the company out of its trouble, they ought to have something to say about its conduct thenceforward till it had discharged its debt to them. "Mr. Westinghouse wastes so much on experimentation, and pays so liberally for whatever he wishes in the way of service and patent rights," said the speaker, "that we are taking a pretty large risk if we give him a free hand with the fund he has asked us to raise. We ought at least to know what he is doing with our money."

· This proposal checked the rising tide, and a second committee was appointed to devise a form of contract which would bind Westinghouse to share with the bankers his knowledge, and to some degree his direction, of his Company's affairs. A new program was drawn up, making the loan contingent upon the bankers' right to name the general manager, and Westinghouse was invited in and asked whether it was satisfactory. With great positiveness, but without any show of resentment, he immediately answered that the concession demanded was too vital for him to consider, and candidly stated his reasons. The bankers expressed their willingness to make a few modifications of their plan, but, as none of these covered his objections, there was some further discussion, and it seemed probable that, if the meeting continued much longer, he would be able to get the money on his own terms; for he clung so firmly to the view that, after all he had done for Pittsburgh, it was only fair that Pittsburgh should do him a good turn when he needed it, as to put compromise out of the question. After a little more futile talk, he announced that he must have a final answer then and there. The bankers gave him one — a flat refusal. Realizing what this meant to him, they waited almost breathlessly to note its effect. To their astonishment, instead of being staggered, he rose with a smile, remarking; "Well, thank God I know the worst at last!" And waiting only long enough to tell them a humorous story in illustration of the unburdening of his mind, he bade them good day and walked out of the room.

That night he took train for New York, and in the morning strode into the banking district there, where his personal acquaintance was limited, and the affairs of the Electric and Manufacturing Company were practically unknown. But every one knew George Westinghouse by reputation, and the fame of his inventions, large as it had become, was not wider than the fame of his resourcefulness and integrity in business.

The results of this errand to the great financial center took several months to mature, but they were momentous, and turned what had seemed a deadly misfortune into an opening for a new and better future. The banking house of August Belmont and Company took the lead in forming a financial syndicate so strong as to command universal confidence. Two electric lighting companies — the United States and the Consolidated — which had for some time been controlled by the Westinghouse interests under lease, were absorbed into the combination, and their stockholders allowed to exchange their present holdings for the new shares of the Westinghouse Electric and Manufacturing Company, preferred and common in certain proportions, while the stockholders of the dominating corporation were asked to surrender forty per cent of their old stock and take second preference shares in the reorganized company in lieu of the remainder. The net result was the reduction of a total outstanding liability of more than ten million dollars, with annual interest charges exceeding one hundred eighty thousand dollars, to less than nine million dollars, all in stock — thanks to a voluntary sacrifice on the part of the stockholders and the willingness of the bankers and creditors concerned to take preferred shares in an enterprise of which the success must depend almost wholly on one man.

This triumph, gratifying as it was, did not stir the sensibilities of Westinghouse half so deeply as the conduct of the employees of his original Electric Company, who, as soon as they learned of the trouble he was in, had come to him with the proposal to work for half pay till he could get upon his feet again. Another incident which had warmed his heart was a visit from T. A. Gillespie, the contractor who drilled his first gas well and had done a good deal of work for him in the past, and whose latest bills were still unpaid. Mr. Gillespie called not only to say that these obligations might be indefinitely postponed, but to offer a loan of thousands of dollars that very day if it would help any. Westinghouse declined all such tenders, but they were not the less pleasing to him as evidence of the esteem in which he was held by men who knew him best on his human side.

It seemed at that period as if every aspiring inventor who hit upon, or dreamed of, a new idea in electric lamps, made it his first business to hunt up Westinghouse as a possible customer. A favorite object of the vagaries of such persons was the filament to be used for incandescent lighting, since a poor one was liable to break with the slightest jar, and even one otherwise good might not endure subjection to the current for any length of time. One lamp, the patent rights for which were acquired through the purchase of the Sawyer-Man Company, formed the basis of expensive lawsuits in the United States courts, culminating in the defeat of Westinghouse, the sole important result of the litigation being to demonstrate which of the features in controversy were already public property. His adversaries in this fight were the Edison interests which later formed the nucleus of the General Electric Company; and, as they had given him so much trouble in New York, it is not unreasonable to suppose that there may have been a bit of the tit-for-tat spirit animating his entrance upon a contest with them in another and more broadly conspicuous field.

The Columbian Exposition, a World's Fair designed to celebrate the four-hundredth anniversary of the discovery of America, was announced to be held in Chicago in 1893, the postponement of a year from the appropriate date being deemed advisable because of the pendency of a Presidential campaign. Sealed proposals had been invited for lighting the fair grounds by electricity, and all the lighting companies realized that the job would afford exceptional advertising opportunities to the contractor whose work should be projected for six months against so artistic a background of architecture, landscape gardening, and water effects. It was the greatest single undertaking in its line that had ever been attempted in this country; by common consent there were only two concerns competent to handle it, the General Electric Company and the Westinghouse Electric and Manufacturing Company; and it was generally understood that the latter was not among the bidders.

When the bids were opened in April, 1892, it was found that the several companies of the General Electric group had put in figures ranging from $13.98 to $18.51 per light. But there was also another bidder whom nobody would have suspected of the temerity to compete with these powerful interests. He was Charles F. Locksteadt, president of the South Side Machine and Metal Works of Chicago, and his offer was $5.49 per light. The big concerns stood aghast. Who was this intruder? Could any one of consequence vouch for his responsibility? Who would manufacture the apparatus for him?

Mr. Locksteadt approached Mr. Westinghouse, hoping to interest him in the situation, and in due course the Westinghouse Electric and Manufacturing Company advised the officials of the Columbian Exposition that it would undertake to carry out the Locksteadt bid. After considerable negotiation it was agreed that new bids be called for. On opening these a bid from the Westinghouse interests of $5.25

per light was found the lowest on the list, and Westinghouse was awarded the contract.

It was, in the judgment of not a few of his friends familiar with the circumstances, a reckless dive in the dark; and in strict truth it was a profitless venture if the only question to be taken into account were its immediate return in dollars and cents. But the inventor's imagination had leaped far enough ahead for him to realize that this was the opportunity of a lifetime for introducing his products to the notice of the whole world, and, as usual, what he paid for such an advantage was a secondary consideration.

After the contract had been signed and sealed, he was faced with a fresh puzzle. He could manufacture all the rest of the equipment needed, but where was he to look for his lamps? The Edison combination, of course, would not sell him any, and they had the patent rights on the only all-glass-globe incandescent lamp in existence. Though the validity of these rights was then a subject of litigation in the federal courts, the decision of the final appeal was probably close at hand, with all the probabilities favoring affirmation. Plainly, the only thing the contractor could do was to devise some new kind of globe or bulb, which, even if not so good as the Edison globe, would suffice for his present purpose.

What his ingenuity presently evolved was the "stopper" lamp — so called because, instead of the one-piece bulb invented by Edison, it was made in two pieces, the one that contained the wire fitting into the mouth of the bulb-shaped one as a cork fits into the mouth of a bottle. Of course, with only such a plug to depend upon, it might prove impossible to exclude the air for long. If so, it would be necessary to renew the bulbs frequently, and this would have to be done by hand at a heavy aggregate cost. But such difficulties were negligible by comparison with the great end to be gained, and the inventor plunged into his task with zeal. He found that he could use soft iron where the Edison lamp used platinum, and in other ways reduce largely the cost of his bulbs. Substantially all the mechanism used in making the new lamps had to be specially designed, and he took a short cut by setting up a glass factory in Allegheny, whither he used to go daily while at home, to instruct the operatives in running the grinding machines so as to make the stoppers as nearly as possible a perfect fit.

The conclusive decision in the all-glass-globe lamp patent suit was in favor of Edison as expected. It was handed down on December 15, 1892, but, thanks to the new invention, caused no disturbance in the plans of the Westinghouse Electric and Manufacturing Company for carrying out the World's Fair contract. An incident did occur, however, which illustrates the dramatic guise the merest chance may assume.

George Westinghouse was in New York City for the Christmas season, and on the afternoon of the twenty-third of December happened to take an up-bound elevated train in company with his friend and legal adviser Charles A. Terry. In their car they encountered Grosvenor P. Lowrey, chief counsel for the Edison Electric Light Company in patent matters, and took seats next to him.   During the conversation that ensued, Mr. Lowrey dropped a casual remark which indicated that Frederick P. Fish, another of the Edison lawyers, was that day in Pittsburgh.   Immediately Westinghouse began to pay close attention to what the speaker was saying, and made two or three half-questioning comments, which in turn appeared to cause Mr. Lowrey some embarrassment, as if it had suddenly struck him that perhaps he had been more communicative than was wise.   At Fourteenth Street, Westinghouse rose, quietly motioned to Terry to do likewise, and the two excused themselves to Lowrey and quitted the train.

Hardly were they alone together on the platform when Westinghouse plumped at Terry the question: "What is Fish doing in Pittsburgh?"

Terry was unable, of course, to offer more than a guess in response.   Both recalled the fact that some of their people had met Fish in New York the day before, and were sure that he uttered no hint of an intended visit to Pittsburgh.

"I can't conceive what would call him there," said Westinghouse, "except to make some new trouble for us.   We shall have to act quickly to head it off, whatever it is.   I wish you'd hunt up Curtis and Kerr at once and let them get to work."   Thomas B. Kerr and Leonard E. Curtis had been his counsel throughout his lamp litigation.

Finding that Curtis had gone to his home in Englewood for the night, Terry sought him there and related the story of the meeting on the train and what had developed from it. Instantly Curtis put himself in touch by wire with George H. Christy, a professional colleague in Pittsburgh, warning him to look out for whatever was in the wind.

The next morning when Mr. Fish entered the United States Circuit Court Room in Pittsburgh, where Judge Acheson was to hold chambers, he was surprised to find Christy seated within the bar. After a brief and rather tense interval of silence, he turned to Christy with the inquiry:

"Have you a case on this morning?"

"Nothing on the calendar," answered Christy blandly; "but I thought I might possibly have something to attend to, so I was just sitting around to await events."

The two lawyers looked each other over with a poor affectation of indifference. Christy was still not quite sure what the other lawyer was there for, though he had his suspicions; while the latter's eyes wandered warily toward a package of papers in Christy's hands, of which he obviously did not like the appearance. Neither had long to wait for larger knowledge. Judge Acheson, immediately after the formal opening of the court, called up a few held-over items of business, and in a moment the secret was out. The Edison Company's counsel had, it appeared, on the day before, applied for a restraining order to prevent the Westinghouse Electric and Manufacturing Company from selling, or otherwise disposing of, its electric lamps, charging it with bad faith in resorting to a technical subterfuge to evade the injunction against the Sawyer-Man lamp. He had hoped to obtain such a restraining order on his presentation of the case; the Judge had expressed a reluctance to issue the order till the other side could be heard, but had yielded to counsel's urgency so far as to consent to take the matter under consideration over night. As a result of Christy's presentation of the facts in the case, the matter was laid over till after Christmas, when the accused company not only satisfied the Court that it was guiltless of any attempt at evasion, but followed up its advantage by producing a set of blue prints to show the details of the construction and operation of the stopper-lamp, which made it plain that this constituted no infringement of the Edison lamp patents. Although more or less harassing warfare was kept up afterward, this unexpected proceeding in court so far cleared the way for Westinghouse that he was able to proceed with the manufacture of his lamps and carry out his great undertaking at Chicago.

As I have suggested, the whole dramatic incident developed from mere chance. Had not Westinghouse and Terry taken the car they did that after noon, they would not have met Lowrey. Had not Lowrey felt confident that Fish had succeeded in his plan that morning, he would have been too cautious to let drop the remark which caught Westinghouse's special attention. Above all, but for the wizard-like keenness of Westinghouse, this remark might have passed as casually as the rest of the conversation. Repeated applications for injunctions, even though ultimately unsuccessful, would have hampered and delayed his work on the Fair grounds, and rendered impossible the first illumination on the date fixed in the contract.   This would have damaged the credit of his company, and it had been a matter of pride with him to prove to the world that since its re-organization it was once more firmly on its feet.

When the World's Fair opened on the 1st of May, 1893, the Westinghouse lighting plant was one of the few very large installations that was complete and in place.   It included twelve dynamos ten feet high and weighing about seventy-five tons apiece, con-structed on the Tesla multiphase system.   Popular interest was divided between these giant machines, the largest of their kind up to that time, and the switchboard.   The latter was made of one thousand square feet of marble and divided into three sections, reached by galleries with spiral iron stairways.   It operated forty circuits, so articulated that, if a break occurred in any circuit, another could be instantly substituted to do its work.   The switchboard con-trolled two hundred and fifty thousand incandescent lamps of sixteen candle power, only one hundred and eighty thousand of which were to be used at one time, the remaining seventy thousand being a reserve against emergencies.   What astonished visitors most, perhaps, was to see this elaborate mechanism handled by one man, who was constantly in touch, by tele-phone or messenger, with every part of the grounds, and responded to requests of all sorts by the mere turning of a switch.

The Fair lasted six months.   It was illuminated every night, and with a success which received an extraordinary tribute.   The currency panic of 1893 had swept over the country and combined with a number of other adverse conditions to reduce receipts; but the management, though badly put to it at times to make both ends meet, decided that, whoever else might have to wait, there was one creditor whose bills they must promptly meet, since by his enterprise and courage he had saved them a round million dollars: that one was George Westinghouse. A special arrangement was therefore made, whereby he was to be paid a certain sum weekly from the current receipts. When the panic was passing through its most acute stage, and the banks were refusing to cash checks because they had nothing to cash them with, the treasury of the Fair handed over to the local representative of the Westinghouse Electric and Manufacturing Company large quantities of dollars and half-dollars and quarters, which were shipped directly to Pittsburgh, and used to pay off the workmen in the shops at a time when currency was commanding five per cent premium.

CHAPTER XIII

FROM NIAGARA TO THE NAVY

GREAT as the World's Fair undertaking was, George Westinghouse was soon to be called to lend a hand at one far greater — the harnessing of Niagara's waters for the industrial uses of mankind; and the demonstration he made at Chicago may have played no small part in the creation of this opportunity.

From their discovery by white explorers early in the sixteenth century, the falls of Niagara had commonly been regarded as a scenic wonder rather than as a potential agent of utility. Now and then, as the era of mechanical invention advanced, would arise a prophet venturesome enough to talk about a day when this and other great cataracts would be made to turn mill wheels and thus help feed the world; but such prognostications rarely inspired any one to attempt their fulfillment; and although between 1847 and 1861 sundry owners of land bordering on the Niagara River diverted water for hydraulic power purposes on a considerable scale, their experiments proved financially unsuccessful, and little more thought was spent on the subject for a number of years. Meanwhile the neighborhood of the falls had suffered so at the hands of vandals that the State government had interfered for the protection of its natural beauties by condemning enough private property to make them the center of a public reservation.

In 1886 Thomas Evershed of Rochester, a division engineer on the Erie Canal, prepared plans for a tunnel about a mile and a half long, running underneath the town of Niagara Falls and parallel to the river above the falls. Near the upper end of the tunnel, canals or shafts were to take water from the river and carry it to pits, in which, at a depth of 150 feet, were to be placed turbine wheels for supplying power. Having served the purpose of turning the wheels, the water would pass into the tunnel, and be carried down to its mouth a short distance below the falls. Factories were to be built within easy reach of the power. And all this would be possible without impairing the picturesqueness of the landscape.

Evershed's diagrams and figures attracted much notice in the vicinage, where several well-to-do residents undertook to raise the sum needed to construct the canals, pits, and tunnel, and install the wheels and other machinery. As a preliminary, they organized the Niagara Falls Power Company and obtained a charter from the State legislature. But the millions required were not readily obtainable in Western New York, and the project had begun to droop when it occurred to William Rankine, a young lawyer, to lay his documents and sketches before Francis Lynde Stetson of New York City, a professional friend with a large clientele among men of wealth. Before their interview was over, Stetson was so impressed that he took the papers and agreed to see what he could do.

In his turn, he opened negotiations with several clients of large means like Darius O. Mills, J. Pierpont Morgan, Edward D. Adams, and Hamilton McK. Twombley. All recognized it as a serious enterprise, and attended with many uncertainties, so far ahead was it of anything of the kind that had been attempted, but they concluded to give it their support. As it was important that whatever favorable results might be obtained should accrue primarily to the projectors, an eligible tract of land adjacent to the river was purchased and laid out for factory sites and a model village; and the Cataract Construction Company was organized to finance and execute the plans finally decided upon.

These plans, it was assumed, would in the main be Evershed's; but experts in various parts of the world were to be called upon to go over them item by item and advise the Company what modifications, if any, were desirable. Up to that point the broad question was still open, whether the utilization of Niagara power could best be accomplished by hydraulic, pneumatic, or electric agencies. In June, 1890, Mr. Adams, who, with his engineering adviser, Doctor Coleman Sellers of Philadelphia, had been passing a good deal of time in London discussing the general subject with English and foreign technologists, organized the so-called International Niagara Commission, with power to award twenty-two thousand dollars in prizes for the most useful ideas.

The commission, which had for its chairman Sir William Thomson, later raised to the peerage as Lord Kelvin, for its secretary Professor William Cawthorne Unwin, Dean of the Central Institute of Guilds of the City of London, and in its membership men of such eminence as Doctor Sellers, Lieutenant Colonel Theodore Turretini of Geneva, and Professor E. Mascart of the College of France, invited the British Westinghouse Electric and Manufacturing Company and sundry other large concerns to submit competitive plans, the principal prize offered being three thousand dollars. Lewis B. Stillwell of the American company, who chanced to be in London at the time, believed that the polyphase alternating current system offered the most practical key to the situation, and was anxious to get permission to put in a bid for the British company, but Westinghouse refused, explaining later that the prize offered was an entirely inadequate sum to pay for one hundred thousand dollars' worth of advice, and adding: "When the Niagara people are ready to do business, we shall make them a proposal."

The Electric and Manufacturing Company had been sadly hampered in its commercial development of the polyphase system during 1890 and 1891 by the financial difficulties with which it had to contend, but in 1892 it constructed two one-hundred-fifty-horse-power rotary converters, and Westinghouse invited the Cataract Construction Company to send its engineers to Pittsburgh to inspect and test these machines. Doctor Sellers and Professor Henry A. Rowland responded, and George Forbes, one of the

foremost electricians of England, came at another
time. All three were much impressed — especially
Forbes, who more than a year before had put himself
on record, in connection with the submission of a
project covering the engineering work on the new
enterprise, in favor of using the alternating current.
But even so eminent an authority was unable to
bring the rest of the Construction Company's ad-
visers to his view, and at the outset all voted to con-
demn and reject the alternating system, except
Forbes himself and an electrician from Buda-Pesth.
Forbes never wavered for a moment, and finally
turned the tide of preference by proving the prohibitive cost of a continuous current installation.
Of the whole group of experts consulted, Lord Kelvin
was the only one who still held out in opposition.
Some time afterward he cabled the Construction
Company, reasserting his loyalty to his original judgment, but admitting that the company "could certainly succeed with the alternating current." And
still later, when practical trials had proved his apprehensions vain, he candidly confessed that the
alternating current "alone solves the problem well
and economically."

On October 24, 1893, as the result of a spirited
competition with the General Electric Company, the
Westinghouse Electric and Manufacturing Company
was awarded a contract for three mammoth generators. Westinghouse took a very active part personally in the direction of the work at Pittsburgh,
and in less than eighteen months the first five-thou-
sand-horse-power turbo-alternator unit operated by

hydraulic power was in place and in working order, with a capacity which proved capable of doing even more than the contract called for, yielding five thousand, one hundred thirty-five horse power — nearly three per cent above the demand.

Meanwhile, in the access of enthusiasm which followed the assurance that something had at last been begun toward utilizing power from the Niagara River, all central New York gave itself up for a time to a revel in electric promotion. Companies were organized on every side to buy and sell locally the power which was to be transmitted from the falls, and plans were drawn for the storage stations which were to serve as media in the scheme. A message of Governor Flower to the legislature had advocated, in the interest of economical transportation, the substitution of electricity for draft mules as a motive power on the Erie Canal, and a law had been passed appropriating ten thousand dollars for experimentation in this field. The State Superintendent of Public Works negotiated with Westinghouse for an equipment for a first test, to cost five thousand dollars if necessary, the State and the inventor dividing the expense equally between them. Trolley wires were strung along the banks, and, as the Niagara project was still all on paper, power for the test was obtained from the Rochester street railway company.

On May 18, 1893, an old canal boat, fitted with apparatus like that on a trolley car, was started for a demonstrative trip of one mile. It passed through locks and around curves, making an average rate of about five miles an hour, or within one mile of the lawful speed limit on canals.   The Governor, several other State officers, and prominent citizens, as well as Westinghouse and some of his leading subordinates, were passengers, and nearly all pronounced the case for electric propulsion well proved.   But there remained a few doubters who protested that, after a boat had been drawn by trolley from Buffalo to the Hudson River, it must still be towed down to New York.   This criticism having been duly threshed out, the thoughts of every one were diverted from trolley propulsion to individual motors, and gradually, after a period of fruitless experiments, interest in the canal project died of inanition.   The Niagara enterprise prospered, however, and for years thereafter the Power Company was a frequent customer of the Westinghouse Electric and Manufacturing Company, which installed unit after unit until ten huge generators were in place, with an aggregate capacity of fifty-five thousand horse power.

Of what has grown out of these beginnings, a few figures will give us a suggestion.   Today there are power houses on the American and Canadian sides having a combined capacity already installed of over two hundred thousand, with additional plants under construction.   By means of transformers situated near the power houses, and the use of overhead and subway lines according to their respective adaptation, electricity is distributed for lighting, power, and heating purposes over nearly the entire western and middle parts of New York State, and as far east as Syracuse.   Development has not yet ceased, and although restricted to some degree by legislation, no one would venture now to define the lengths to which it may go before it ceases. The city of Niagara Falls, which contained about ten thousand population when ground was first broken for the mammoth power enterprise, has now thirty-five thousand, and in the same interval its real estate has increased in assessed valuation from seven million to thirty-two million dollars. Most of this advance can reasonably be attributed to the influence, direct and indirect, of the industrial awakening due to the Niagara power enterprise. In what measure the neighboring communities affected have profited likewise is less readily determined, as they have had other resources than the great waterfall to draw upon.

As an illustration of the versatility of Westinghouse's mind, it is worth noting that, in the midst of all the hubbub attendant upon the reorganization of his Electric company, the crisis in the lamp controversy, the lighting of the World's Fair, and the installations at Niagara, he never became so absorbed in any of these concerns as to let his interest slacken in others. His experience in building up a natural gas industry in Pittsburgh had moved him to study the possibilities of the production of economical power by the use of a gas engine, since its efficiency as a prime mover when using natural gas was far superior to that of the best steam engines of that period. Even with a manufactured fuel gas, containing less heat than natural gas, there was a decided advantage in respect to the cost of fuel when used in a gas engine. But gas engines had not then been designed of sufficient size to meet the requirements for large powers necessary for their advantageous use, particularly for the production of electricity, and their speed regulation was not sufficiently accurate to produce the uniform rotary motion necessary for the production of electric current. In his usual energetic and comprehensive manner, he designed and successfully built gas engines of more than three hundred horse power with a system of regulation that furnished a uniform rotative speed, thus solving the problem of the successful production of electric current by gas-engine power. The gas-engine development ultimately resulted in the manufacture, by the Westinghouse Machine Company, of engines of more than five thousand horse power that found their principal uses in blast furnaces and rolling mills.

Westinghouse had given a great deal of attention to the subject of the manufacture of fuel gas from coal, and in connection with the gas-engine development he designed and built experimentally many forms of gas producers, seeking to develop a type that would make gas from soft coal by a process which avoided the many difficulties arising from the by-products and impurities contained in the coal. As the result of years of effort, he finally evolved a form that met demands in a very practical way. In his larger effort, however, to discover a process for manufacturing gas at a cost and of a quality that could be profitably sold and distributed in competition with coal for heating and power purposes, he was not successful.

A notion Westinghouse kept in mind in perfecting the gas engine was that it would one day supplant the steam engine because of its great fuel economy, comparative freedom from offensive qualities, and the ease with which, in connection with apparatus for generating and conveying an electric current, the engine and producer could be placed wherever coal could most conveniently be received and stored. He thought that by setting up generating stations, with gas engines, at intervals of ten or twenty miles, long railroads could be run by electricity; and an electric locomotive capable of hauling twenty or thirty cars could thus be operated by one man, with a current simultaneously used for lighting tracks, running machinery and shops, pumping water, handling freight at stations, lighting and heating trains, and the like.

The subject of electrifying street railroads, also, strongly stirred his interest at this juncture. The popular demand for rapid transit was loud in every large city. Cable lines had fallen into disfavor; overhead trolleys were unsightly, and no satisfactory underground system had yet been reduced to what seemed reasonable bounds of cost. But an unperfected invention had been brought to his notice which he spent a good deal of time and thought in developing. It was commonly known as the "button system", because its visible factors were the button-like heads of iron pins which appeared in pairs at seven-foot intervals between the tracks, raised a trifle above the surface of the roadway. Every pair were connected with electrical conductors, leading to electro-magnetic switches alongside of the track, which in their turn were connected with a main

electric line laid in a conduit just beneath the pave-
ment and fed from a power station like a trolley.
Under every car were carried two iron bars, projecting
from its bottom like the prongs of a tuning fork;
and only when these bars were in contact with two
corresponding buttons was the circuit completed
that propelled the car. At all other times the buttons
were inert and harmless. The button system had
the advantage of the underground trolley now so
widely used, that it required no greater depth of
excavation than the ties.

While he was studying this device, the directors
of the Manhattan Elevated Railway system began
discussing the question of changing its motive power
from steam to electricity, and a majority inclined
strongly to such a change if they could have any
assurance of what would be the wisest plan of electrification to adopt. Westinghouse was consulted
by Russell Sage, but, firmly as he believed that electrification of all railways was coming in due season,
he was loath to advise an early change. Just what
he had in mind in discouraging immediate action
did not at once appear, though later he brought out
his idea of using gas engines for running the generators. The matter was postponed as he suggested;
a few years afterward it was taken up with him again,
he having in the interval received a contract for
equipping an underground trolley for the Third
Avenue surface railway, which had been run by cable.
When the Manhattan directors had finally decided
what they wanted, they called upon him to submit
plans for the heavy generating machinery for a new

power house, and for the apparatus for substations. Other large manufacturers and contractors were invited to do the same; but the Westinghouse plans, after a searching analysis by a board of engineering experts, were accepted as the best offered, and won the award of a contract mounting well up into the millions, and calling among other things for eight three-phase alternating generators of six thousand six hundred fifty horse-power capacity apiece — the largest ever constructed till then. The alternating current was to be conveyed from the main power house to the substations, and there reduced by step-down converters to a direct current of five hundred volts for feeding to a third rail.

The third rail never found an enthusiastic champion in Westinghouse. Though appreciating its great possibilities as a means of propelling trains, he was always mindful of its menace to human life. Since it was going to be used in any event, he suggested its division into sections, with provisions for the automatic supply of the requisite current to these in turn, as the train moved. Even with such precautions he regarded the rail as only a dangerous makeshift, and insisted that what the elevated roads ought to have done was to use the overhead trolley instead — not the fragile and disfiguring construction too commonly met with, but a substantially built line, of inoffensive appearance. The managers of the Manhattan railway were not ready to credit his apprehensions. Time has pretty well demonstrated that this was one of the rare instances where his matured judgment in the electrical manufacturing field was at fault; and to this day the third rail continues the Manhattan's sole dependence for motive power.

In spite of activities such as these, Westinghouse still found time to examine the merits of a type of steam turbine developed by the Honorable Charles Algernon Parsons of London, and ultimately obtained authority to manufacture under the Parsons patents in the United States. It will be recalled that the first invention patented by Westinghouse was a rotary engine, and throughout his life, until the last ten or twelve years, he devoted much time and thought as well as large sums of money to an effort to produce an engine of the rotary type that would meet his ideals with respect to efficiency, simplicity, and cheap production. His efforts did not cease until he became interested in the steam turbine, in which he recognized a form of rotary steam engine that solved his problem of so many years.

In its earlier stages, the Parsons turbine had been used to drive electric generators for the purpose of lighting ships, and, about the time that Westinghouse procured the foreign rights, Parsons had fitted a vessel called the *Turbinia* with one of his engines from which remarkable speed performances were obtained, thus indicating its possible adaptation to further marine purposes. The Parsons designs purchased by Mr. Westinghouse were the result of English practice, and not adapted to the conditions under which it was desired to develop this type of prime mover in the United States. Under Westinghouse's direction, important constructional changes were made and suitable electric generators designed, so that the combined outfit was put upon the market to supply electricity for light and power. In the original form the speeds of the Parsons machines had been very high and their efficiency rather low; in the form developed by Westinghouse, both features were so improved that the machines compared favorably with the best type of reciprocating steam engine in the matter of efficiency, weighed much less, occupied much smaller space, and required less care and attention in their operation.

The development of the steam turbine in the last few years has been accompanied by almost astounding results. Single units of more than 75,000 horse power are in operation and still larger sizes in contemplation. The thermal efficiency of the later machines has reached a point which engineers not many years ago regarded as unattainable. The results in gains to the public at large from these advances are of marked value, as evidenced by the wide extension of distributed electric power at relatively low cost, so that many forms of mechanism of great utility and contributing to domestic comfort are made available. For practically all purposes, other forms of prime movers have been displaced as the result of the availability of cheap and convenient electric power. The gas engine, which at one time seemed to have an important future, has been for the present relegated to a minor position in the matter of power production.

One of the possibilities which impressed the mind of Westinghouse in developing the turbine for marine uses was this: if the same propulsive power could be got from an engine occupying only a fraction of the space required by the engines then in use in ships, there would be more room for the coal bunkers, which in turn meant a wider steaming radius, letting a vessel stay longer out of port without resorting to coaling at sea; and if these advantages could be obtained without the vibration or thumping of reciprocating engines, the machinery would last longer and would need less frequent repairs. In order to make sure that he was on the right track, he called into consultation Rear-Admiral Melville, a retired engineer-in-chief of the navy, and one of his most experienced associates, John H. Macalpine, and set them to work at a laborious investigation of the whole subject.

Their first report was not encouraging. The trouble with the turbine was that it did not too little, but altogether too much. Its greatest economic efficiency, they said, was at high speed, whereas that of the propeller was at a comparatively low rate of revolution. If the propeller were driven too fast, it simply cut holes in the water instead of pushing the ship along; but to reduce the speed of the turbine below a certain degree involved a great waste of energy, and to drop it still lower rendered it incapable of running the propeller. So the problem narrowed down to the discovery of a means of using a high-speed engine to drive a low-speed propeller and yet conserve the force of both to the utmost.

This Melville and Macalpine accomplished by an invention that made practicable the use of gearing to connect the turbine with the propeller shaft, the gears being so proportioned as to permit each element to run at its most efficient speed.   While gearing had formerly been employed to a limited extent for somewhat similar purposes, no general success had attended the effort to make it applicable to the large powers necessary in marine propulsion.   The Melville-Macalpine system employs what is technically described as a "floating frame", one element of the general arrangement that carries the pinions transmitting the power from the turbine to the main gears driving the propeller.   The floating frame is so designed as automatically to maintain perfect alignment between the teeth of the pinions and gears, the working pressures of the contacting teeth being thus limited to a degree that prevents destructive wear. The Machine Company, under the direction of Westinghouse, built an experimental set of gears capable of transmitting seventy-five hundred horse power. These operated successfully, and, when placed in the United States collier *Neptune*, realized all the expectations of the inventors and of Westinghouse, who had made important contributions to the basic scheme.

Since this successful installation, the use of gears has become almost universal in the newer naval vessels, and their employment in connection with the highly efficient steam turbines now available marks a most important advance in the art of marine propulsion.   It is worth noting, moreover, that the experimental development of the Melville-Macalpine invention was carried on by Mr. Westinghouse during the receivership period of the Machine Company, against the strong opposition of the engineering and financial directors of the Company at that time.

There was included in the *Neptune* experiment, a most ingenious invention of H. T. Herr, Vice President of the Machine Company, by means of which the pilot or steersman was given entire control over the propelling machinery without the intervention of manual operation in the engine room.   The operations of starting, stopping, speed regulation, and reversing were effected directly from the pilot house; and, though the mechanism worked as designed, the innovation was so radical that it was regarded askance by most naval men, who knew only the old method of giving the engineer his orders through speaking tubes and bells.   It will be taking no great risk in prophecy to assert that the more modern method of control will presently come into general use.   Its advantages, particularly in the manipulation of vessels engaged in battle or threatened with collision, are obvious even to the popular mind.   In not a few respects it parallels on the water the instantaneous mastery of his train by the locomotive driver in his cab, with the lever of his air brake within reach of his hand.

CHAPTER XIV

"Blushing Honors Thick Upon Him"

As we have already seen, George Westinghouse had no notion of confining his activities to the country of his home, but from the hour of his first success began to lay plans covering the civilized world. Wherever he saw a possible opening, however remote, he lost no time about arranging for its occupation. In this way, while keeping Pittsburgh for their permanent base, his various industries established outposts in all the leading countries of Europe.

As early as 1888 he had obtained a contract for an electric plant capable of lighting a considerable area in London. Everything for this purpose was manufactured in Pittsburgh and shipped over. Other contracts which followed, extending into various lines of electrical equipment, were handled in the same way. By 1897 the English orders had mounted in multitude so as to arouse an inquiry in both countries whether the supplies could not be more promptly and economically furnished if there were a factory on the ground, especially as England was taking kindly to rapid transit by trolley on the American plan, and the Westinghouse Electric and Manufacturing Company was recognized as a source from which to procure the very latest inventions. A group of prominent Englishmen interested in engineering enterprises accepted directorships in the British branch, which was enlarged in scope and heavily capitalized, and a tract of about one hundred and thirty acres of land was bought at Trafford Park, on the outskirts of Manchester, adjoining the ship canal and with abundant railroad facilities, as a site for the works. These were to cover thirty acres under roof; and, as it was a part of Westinghouse's plan to house his men as well as hire them, a building company laid out a somewhat smaller tract near by as a residence town.

Under the new organization, the British company was to receive from the American company the rights for the British Empire, exclusive of Canada, in all the Westinghouse electric patents then existing, and all that might be issued during the following ten years. The two corporations were to coöperate in every way. The articles of incorporation of the British company were made so broad as to include power to conduct pretty nearly any sort of business it wished to, from running a hotel and renting dwellings to managing schools and banks, so that, in standing sponsor for its undertakings, the American company was laying itself liable to a good many vicissitudes.

Though assigning the supervision of the plans and the preparation of the estimates to his own engineers, Westinghouse made a strong point, from politic considerations, of having only British labor employed in the actual work of building the shops. A Manchester contractor was engaged to lay the foundations, and a London contractor to put up the steel framework, but neither was willing to predict when his share of the task would be finished. Several weeks passed before the first spadeful of earth was turned, and fully six months before the foundations had reached a stage where the steel men could attack the superstructure. Meanwhile the orders were piling up, and the dates fixed when they must be filled left only eighteen months' leeway for rearing nine huge buildings. The situation was exasperating. Winter was drawing near, and the best the contractors would venture to guess was five years for the completion of the job. Then something happened.

Coming over from New York to Pittsburgh one night, Westinghouse found on his train James C. Stewart, a member of a contracting firm who had performed some wonderfully rapid and effective services for him in the past, and in the course of their conversation the Trafford Park delays came up for comment. On arriving in Pittsburgh the following morning, Stewart went at once to Westinghouse's office and looked over the plans. He seemed to see something deliciously humorous in the five-years' suggestion of the British contractors.

"With the right management," was his verdict, after a little calculation, "there is no reason why that work should take more than fifteen months."

"Would you undertake to finish it in that time?" asked Westinghouse.

"On my own terms — yes."

The terms were such as to insure to Stewart rather magnificent profits, but Westinghouse accepted his proposal. He had now got hold of a man after his own heart, and a contract was signed at once. This was in January, 1901. Stewart caught the next steamer for Liverpool, landing on the twenty-fourth. He had never been in England before, but he hastened to Manchester, looked over the ground, and cabled to two of his best American assistants to join him. Though a thousand miles apart when his message reached them, they met aboard ship on the first of February. When their vessel stopped off Queenstown they learned that Stewart was about starting back to America to get his mechanical supplies, so they hired a tender and went out to meet him. As his steamer came up, there he was, leaning over the rail. In another minute there landed on their deck a fat package of papers, which on opening they discovered to be their working orders written out to the minutest detail, so that when they reached Manchester the next day they had only to hasten to Trafford Park and plunge into their task.

Stewart was absent from England three weeks. By that time he had collected the American machinery and implements he needed, and ten more assistants — young men whom he had thoroughly trained in his way of doing business. With his little staff he went at things in true Yankee fashion. A month or more the whole party worked not only all day but far into the night, snatching a bite of food how and when they could, and contenting themselves with four or five hours' sleep in order to rise at six and repeat the performance.

It was a strenuous life, but it paid. The laborers at work when Stewart took hold numbered less than two hundred and fifty; within a month he had a force of twenty-five hundred which he gradually increased to nearly four thousand. He looked after everything personally, substituting American methods for British wherever time could be saved. He ran a line of track from the nearest railway freight station to the grounds, and spurs of this into every building, thus bringing in between two and three hundred carloads of material a day. He furnished the steel workers with automatic riveters to supersede the tedious manual labor they had been doing, and thus more than quadrupled their speed. He replaced the human hodcarriers with steam hoists for lifting bricks and mortar to any story of the buildings, and showed the bricklayers with his own hands how to lay from eighteen hundred to twenty-five hundred brick a day instead of the five or six hundred they had been accustomed to lay, paying them a penny an hour more than their usual wages when they imitated him. By a little encouragement distributed here and there, he managed to infuse into the whole undertaking so much of the spirit which characterized all Westinghouse work at home, that he had eight of the nine buildings ready for occupancy in ten months, and the ninth as soon as some belated changes in the plans made it possible.

When it is remembered that there entered into the construction twelve million feet of lumber, ten million brick, fifteen thousand tons of steel, one hundred seventy-five thousand feet of glass, and forty thousand square yards of paving; that the cost ran well above a million dollars, of which British wage-earners received the largest benefit; that the whole performance under American direction consumed less than one fifth of the time estimated for it by the British contractors consulted; and that the first big job to which the new establishment addressed itself was the electrification of the Metropolitan District and Underground Railways of London — an improvement of which the gross cost was twenty-five million dollars — it seems scarcely wonderful that the press of the world was soon ringing with "the Westinghouse Invasion of England."

Many honors came to George Westinghouse in the course of his busy life. Union College, his alma mater, conferred upon him the degree of Doctor of Philosophy. The Koenigliche Technische Hochschule of Berlin made him a Doctor of Engineering. France took him into her Legion of Honor, King Humbert decorated him with the Order of the Crown of Italy, and he received the Order of Leopold of Belgium from the hands of King Leopold II in person. The Franklin Institute, within a few years of his first success, awarded him the Scott premium and medal for his improvements in air brake construction. He was the first American to receive from the Society of German Engineers the Grashof medal, which is considered in Germany the highest honor that can be conferred upon an engineer. He was the second recipient of the John Fritz medal, the first having been Mr. Fritz himself. He was one of the two honorary members of the American Association for the Advancement of Science. He belonged to a large number of scientific and technological societies, and was called to the presidency of some of them. His immersion in his work, together with his native modesty, moved him to decline more such offices than he accepted, and also to flee from honorary degrees offered him by sundry American colleges in which he was in no way interested.

One of the things he most dreaded in connection with the acceptance of such dignities was making a speech. In May, 1905, the International Railway Congress met in Washington. As it embraced delegates from forty-eight countries besides our own, as it held its meetings only once in five years, and as this was its first visit to the United States, the occasion was regarded as of great importance, and the desire was universal that the American citizen most widely known for his practical achievements for the safety, speed, and comfort of rail transportation should be its chairman. George A. Post of New York, President of the Railway Business Association, was deputed to convey the invitation. Mr. Westinghouse received it with evidences of genuine dismay, especially when he found that he must open the sessions with a formal address. He declared that he could not make a speech to such an audience — he should be tongue-tied with fright.

As he resisted all ordinary arguments, Mrs. Westinghouse was called upon to lend her aid, and held her ground so pertinaciously that he capitulated. Even after he had written the speech he brought it to Mr. Post to look over and criticize.

"His manuscript," said Mr. Post, in narrating the incident to me, "was a fine piece of work from the point of view of comprehensiveness and clarity of expression; but I promptly drew his attention to the fact that it ignored, except for a brief passing reference, the momentous subject of the introduction of electricity as an agency of transportation.

"'I have been personally so involved in that movement,' he answered, 'that I feared it might seem like egotism for me to enlarge upon it.'

"I induced him, nevertheless, to rewrite enough of the address to treat the missing topic as it deserved. When he handed back the revised product he was still suffering from premonitory stage-fright. 'I feel weaker and weaker as the time approaches,' said he; 'I really don't see how I am going to get through this speech.'

"He took comfort from my suggestion that, instead of attempting to commit his remarks to memory, he read them; and the opening day found him as composed as if he were going to one of his own directors' meetings. Even had he not been heartened by my assurances, he could not have helped being affected by what followed his ascent of the platform. The audience he was facing was well sprinkled with men whose aristocratic or academic titles had been blazoned far and wide. This furnished me a pretext for presenting him, by subtle contrast, as 'one who needs neither prefix nor affix to his name — George Westinghouse.' The storm of applause and cheers which greeted him as he stepped forward spoke for itself in point of sincerity."

Of all the tributes paid him in this line, I suspect that two stood a trifle apart from the rest as giving him peculiar pleasure. One was a little paragraph which appeared in *Life* in October, 1899, in a department it was publishing weekly under the heading, "Popular Birthdays":

GEORGE WESTINGHOUSE, BORN OCT. 6, 1846
My dear Mr. Westinghouse:

This is just a brief line sent to you in hopes that it will reach you promptly on the morning of your birthday. Men like you are of more value to a State than others I could mention — but why spoil a happy day by making comparisons? Your creations are like works of art — not only give pleasure, but have a practical value. Where Shakespeare wrought in words, you work in iron and steel. It is good to think of you alive and with us yet, and may Time deal kindly with one whose name is above reproach.

With many congratulations, believe me

Ever yours,

LIFE.

Coming "out of the blue", as it were, from a journal with which he had no relation, the genuinely friendly spirit of this note warmed his heart. The other tribute was of a wholly different character — nothing less than the award, in 1912, by the American Institute of Electrical Engineers, of the

Edison gold medal for "meritorious achievements in the development of the alternating current system." That after a quarter-century of strife, he should receive such a recognition with the name of his great antagonist attached to it, founded on his success in the very field where they had fought their hardest battle, seemed indeed the crowning triumph of his career as a pioneer in the industrial utilization of electricity in America.

From the catalogue of honors must not be omitted two others which emphasize certain qualities more important than technical skill or resourcefulness, scientific learning or prophetic vision. In an earlier chapter, mention was made of the Philadelphia Company, which, thanks to the breadth of its charter, began as a natural gas distributing corporation and gradually absorbed a large share of the public utilities of Pittsburgh. At a stage in its affairs when all the conditions seemed ripe, an offer came to Mr. Westinghouse, through a New York banking house, for the purchase of his controlling interest at a price well above the current market quotations, but he refused to sell unless the minority stockholders were given the chance to sell their shares at an equal price. Then he announced this to the minority, telling them that they need not sell unless they wished to, but that those who were satisfied with the price might make over their stock to him, and he would sell it with his own. In less than three days, more than two thirds of the remaining shares were locked up in his safe. As soon as he had all the stock in his custody, he carried it to New York, met the prospective purchasers, and laid before them a statement of the affairs of the Company. They accepted his word without any examination of the books, and took over his whole budget of certificates at the price originally offered. This exhibition of confidence by the parties on both sides of the bargain attracted wide attention at the time, and has often since been cited in connection with a later episode of kindred significance.

Early in 1905, underwriting circles throughout the country were startled by a scandal which broke out in New York, involving charges of abuse of trust by the officers of some of the great life insurance companies. It was precipitated by the death of Henry B. Hyde, the largest shareholder in the Equitable Life Assurance Society, which was then conducted as an ordinary joint stock company. For some time a violent struggle had been going on for mastery in the management between the Hyde party, which claimed the exclusive right, by virtue of its stock ownership, and another called the Alexander party, representing the policy holders, who claimed that, as their annual contribution furnished the means for running the business, they should have supreme authority in its administration. A crisis in this controversy set afoot inquiries which presently made plain the need for a general overhauling of the local life insurance traffic. Governor Higgins sent a special message on the subject to the legislature, which responded by appointing a commission of investigation. The commission chose as its counsel Charles E. Hughes, whose adroit examination of witnesses unearthed a mass of shocking evidence and incidentally won him a national reputation.

It was shown, among other things, that trust funds had been used for procuring desired legislation, and for speculation in securities designed for the companies' investments; that one insurance officer held directorships in several railroad and other companies, traceable to his control over his own company's investment funds; that well-known attorneys were receiving annual salaries as retainers, without rendering any compensatory service; that agents were indulging in all sorts of trickery, such as accepting potatoes from farmers and passes from railroad men in payment of premiums, taking notes instead of money and making no effort to collect them, and allowing rebates under conditions which opened an endless vista of fraud.

Even before these revelations of corruption had been formally spread upon the record, popular suspicion had become so strong that many shareholders in the Equitable, both in this country and in Europe, had disposed of their stock at a sacrifice, and the new business of the Society was falling off so that its bankruptcy seemed inevitable. At this juncture Thomas Fortune Ryan, the New York financier, came to the rescue. He formed a syndicate to purchase control of the Society, with its four hundred million dollars' worth of accumulated·assets and its six hundred thousand policyholders, and announced his purpose of reorganizing it on a mutual basis. It was a bold stroke, but probably the only one which could save the day not merely for the Equitable but for American life insurance generally; for, in view of the peculiar nature of the interests involved, with their possibilities of disaster for thousands of helpless widows and orphans, the upgrowth of adverse sentiment was taking on the aspect of a great public calamity.

But how was Mr. Ryan to stem so violent a tide? If he kept the control of the Society in his own hands, how many people would believe that he had any higher motive in buying it than a desire to turn the purchase to his personal profit as promptly as possible? Before paying a dollar of the price, he had thought out his plan for putting the policyholders in control of the Society, working to this end through a board of three trustees — men whose names would silence all cavil, and in whom he could afford to vest an extraordinary prerogative. They were to hold the unrestricted power to vote the stock, to prepare the necessary amendments to the charter, to supervise every stage of the reorganization, and be answerable to the public for its cleanness of design, and to choose thirty of the fifty-two directors, leaving the stockholders to elect the remaining twenty-two. For two members of his triumvirate, he selected Grover Cleveland, the only living ex-President of the United States, and Morgan J. O'Brien, who had been for nearly twenty years a highly esteemed Justice of the Supreme Court of the State and was then presiding over its appellate division. As to the third member he consulted with several friends whose judgment he held most in respect. In view of the two selections already made, he did not care about a public officer or a learned lawyer; his hope was to find a business man known throughout the world for intelligence, courage, energy, force of character, and, above everything else, unimpeachable honesty. The man who, of all considered by him and his friends, seemed to meet best this composite demand, was George Westinghouse.

The messenger chosen to convey to Mr. Westinghouse the request for his services was Paul D. Cravath, who had been one of his chief legal counsel for years, and whose intimate friendship with him, it was thought, would make for his acceptance of his trust. A less propitious season for such a proposal it would have been hard to choose. The business of the Electric and Manufacturing Company had expanded so rapidly that its executive resources were overtaxed, and more and more of its president's time and thought and financial credit were continually required to carry things along. Almost any other man than Mr. Westinghouse would have been overwhelmed by the load of responsibility which was heaping upon his single pair of shoulders, and would have insisted upon throwing some of it off rather than taking more on. Mr. Cravath, in presenting Mr. Ryan's request, made no secret of the seriousness of the burden which the trustees would have to assume. With all the facts before him, the argument that finally won Mr. Westinghouse's consent to serve was one based on his duty as a good citizen to put aside his personal preferences in the presence of a crisis with which, for some reason, he was regarded as especially fitted to cope.

Within a week the trustees met, organized, and laid out their general scheme of work. There were several vacancies to be filled in the board of directors, and, as these had been caused by the resignations of James J. Hill, August Belmont, Henry C. Frick, Jacob H. Schiff, John A. Stewart, Andrew J. Cassatt, and other men of like substance, the importance of finding successors of business prominence was obvious. More than two hundred names came up for review, a few of the best suggestions emanating from a little group of policyholders who had banded together to do their utmost for the salvation of the Society. The trustees were occasionally put to their trumps by the need of rapid action. One candidate, for instance, lived in a far Southern State, but possessed natural qualities and a fund of experience so admirably suited to the work he would have to do that the trustees were a unit in their desire to secure him. A search of the lists, however, showed that he lacked an essential requisite: he was not a policyholder. Fortunately, this was a fault that could be quickly remedied; and, between the hours of eleven in the morning and two in the afternoon on the day of the discovery, the gentleman made his formal application, underwent his examination, and had his policy issued, thanks to the activity of the trustees and other officers of the company and the liberal employment of the telegraph.

The soundness of Mr. Ryan's judgment in the choice of his triumvirate was amply proved. For the three years preceding Mr. Cleveland's death their action on nearly all questions brought before them was unanimous, and where they differed in opinions it was a mutually respectful difference, and not on vital matters. The faith of the public in their high qualifications was shown when, preparatory to the first election, they sent out to every policy-holder two papers with carefully couched explanations of the meaning and force of each — a blank ballot, and a proxy containing their own names; for of the ninety thousand responses, only forty-five hundred made any use of the ballot, the others containing signed proxies committing the whole business to the discretion of the trustees.

CHAPTER XV

A Second Financial Ordeal

AFTER so many years of success in overcoming the difficulties that confronted him in building up his organizations, George Westinghouse was destined to suffer the reaction which is due from time to time in all evolutionary processes. We have seen how his Electric and Manufacturing Company passed through the ordeal of the early '90's and came out triumphant. But its very prosperity at a time when the general business of the country was most depressed involved it in fresh perils by begetting overconfidence.

To enlarge its resources, it first increased its capital stock; then it issued collateral trust bonds, later debenture bonds, and later still collateral trust notes; till, with its multiplication of fixed charges, its extraordinarily liberal dividend policy, the maturing of many of its short-term obligations, and the advances it was compelled to make to protect its foreign dependencies — none of which, except the Canadian concern, was on a paying basis — the percentage of net profits to capital declined year after year at an alarming rate. This was not a sign of collapsing traffic: on the contrary, it was due to the steady expansion of the Company's business. The era of electrical development had set in with abnormal energy. More light and power and traction companies were organizing than could be readily financed; and when those of a strictly local character found themselves unable to market their securities on reasonable terms, they had to fall back upon the manufacturing companies from whom they were buying their equipment, settling their purchases only partly in cash, and giving notes for the balance with a deposit of their own stocks and bonds as collateral.

Thus it came about that, with its trade continually on the increase, the Electric and Manufacturing Company was faced with a perilous embarrassment. The banks had been overloaded with the negotiable paper of the small concerns, and began to retrench on their discounts. In accordance with his habit in forecasting the future, Westinghouse read in these phenomena only their hopeful portent. The enormous diffusion of the uses of electricity, and the rapid cheapening of methods for producing it, pointed, for him, to a near day when it should penetrate every branch of industry, public and private. What his prophetic vision overlooked was the ever-increasing need of the means of sustenance for this growth. Unfortunately for him, the men who controlled those means were unable to share his optimism as to the ultimate prospect.

During all this period there was not only no shrinkage in the Company's dividends, but a positive inflation. The rate on both preferred and common stock, starting at seven per cent, rose first to nine and then to ten per cent. Naturally this increased the speculative value of the stocks, but it had the concurrent effect of diminishing the ratio of working capital to volume of trade. For example, the prosperous year ending March 31, 1907, showed a profit applicable to dividends approximating two million eight hundred thousand dollars, but the dividends at the prevailing high rate ate up almost two million and a half of this, leaving less than three hundred thousand dollars with which to tide over the first exigencies of the fiscal year. In the meantime the loans needed were obtained from the banks with more and more difficulty and at a greater and greater cost; an issue of fifteen million dollars of convertible debenture bonds, made in 1906, had been launched only at a net discount of nearly six per cent. As the floating debt continued to rise, resort was had to a new issue of stock, which was offered to the existing shareholders at fifty per cent above par — a premium ostensibly justified by the ten per cent dividend which the Company was then paying and announced its purpose to maintain. But the effort was ineffective, for clouds were already gathering thick on the financial horizon, premonitory of the storm which was to break in the autumn and sweep over the entire country.

The middle of October, 1907, found the Company in actual straits. On the fifteenth it paid its usual quarterly dividend; but a fresh stock issue on which it had counted to bring seven and a half million dollars into its treasury had yielded only about one third of that sum, and, in order to accomplish even this, Westinghouse and one or two other large stock-

holders had been obliged to come forward and practically divide the subscription among them.   It was
carrying a bond burden of some thirty million dollars ;
most of its floating debt of fourteen million dollars
was due or approaching maturity ; and in view of the
situation the banks in Pittsburgh and elsewhere were
refusing any extension of time on the nine million
dollars or more they had advanced, while the creditors for merchandise furnished were pressing their
claims, aggregating about five million dollars, for
payment.   Behind all these direct obligations stood
the consideration due to the stockholders, whose
interest amounted in round numbers to twenty-nine
million dollars, almost all the shares having been
bought at prices above par.

On the eighteenth, Westinghouse, who was in New
York, telegraphed his financial secretary, Walter
Uptegraff, to meet him there, and their canvass of
the whole matter led to the conclusion that, unless
the outstanding loans could be renewed or four million dollars in cash raised at once, the company must
go to the wall.   New York was out of the question
as a further source of assistance, so they hastened
back to Pittsburgh and called into consultation
Judge J. H. Reed, an old and good friend.   Reed
made straight for the local bankers, setting the actual
facts before them as to the inherent strength of the
Company, and enlarging on the economic unwisdom,
on public grounds alone, of letting so magnificent an
asset of the city suffer damage for lack of the means
needed to relieve a momentary pressure.   For twenty-
four hours there seemed a chance that the threatened

catastrophe might be averted. Then came the twenty-second, with its news that the Knickerbocker Trust Company in New York had failed, and that the money center of the country was in the throes of a panic. On the twenty-third, therefore, the directors of the Electric and Manufacturing Company applied to the United States Circuit Court for the appointment of receivers.

After the event, of course, there were a multitude of wiseacres in the neighborhood who shook their heads solemnly and said they had long felt certain of what was coming. The rest of the community, outside of banking circles, was taken by surprise. It had been the policy of the founder and president of the Company to waive needless formalities, and, as most of his fellow shareholders had appeared entirely content with his administration, he had not taken the trouble to advertise its details to the world. No report beyond a mere generality or two had been issued between 1897 and 1907, nor had any regular stockholders' meeting been held during the same period except in 1906. On that occasion a handful of persons present, led by a prominent broker, demanded explanations of sundry transactions of the Company which had taken place on the authority of a special meeting of stockholders and directors: one was an issue of new stock and another the purchase of a small railroad. Westinghouse himself was absent when the colloquy took place, and Vice-President Herr, who was in the chair, assured the dissenters that the reason the Company did not issue more elaborate reports was because it preferred not to expose its inner affairs to the scrutiny of its business rivals.

At the 1907 meeting, however, Westinghouse presided, and invited all who were seeking information to interrogate him. In response to their inquiries he explained that the issue of additional stock mentioned the year before had been made because the Company was receiving orders of such magnitude that it must have more cash in hand to execute them. He added frankly that, borrowing when the money market was exceptionally tight, it had been charged inordinate rates for the accommodation. As to the railroad purchased, it was a valuable property, the securities of which had been taken over as part of a large transaction that resulted to the advantage of the Company. The questioners were very complimentary afterward in their references to the candor of his statement, and an incident which at first threatened to cause an insurrection was closed.

However astute any outsiders may have been, there were members of the inner circle of the Company's management to whom the news of its embarrassment came almost without warning. One was Vice President Herr. At half-past five on the afternoon of the twenty-second of October, he was talking over a routine matter with Westinghouse, who appeared as composed as usual; and as they finished their conversation Westinghouse remarked:

"Herr, I shall have a new job for you to-morrow."

"What's that?" asked Herr.

"Receiver of the Electric Company."

Overnight, the news filtered out in various directions, but some persons who heard it found it difficult to credit when they saw all the men busy the next day at their usual tasks, and the chief wearing an unclouded brow. At half-past nine in the morning, while his counsel were preparing the final papers for presentation to the court, one of his lieutenants called to see him about a matter of current business. When it was disposed of, he exclaimed as buoyantly as if financial straits were the subject furthest from his mind: "By the way, Macfarland, I've got an idea now for our turbine that will make a sensation when we bring it out!"

Nevertheless it proved a stirring day in the chief's own office in the Westinghouse Building. Telegraph boys were scurrying back and forth, the telephone bell kept up an unceasing clatter, and visitors would run in for a brief interview and out again with equal haste.

Westinghouse saw those with whom he felt he could speak freely, but excused himself to any whom he suspected of coming chiefly from motives of curiosity. To all who inquired about the situation he said the same thing in effect: "The Company is not insolvent — only hampered for the moment. It is doing more business than ever before. It will come out all right." And to an old friend whose voice had a particularly despondent inflection he counseled calmness, adding: "I grant you that this is not pleasant, but it isn't the biggest thing in the world. All large business has its ups and downs. The crisis through which we are passing is only part of our day's work."

Whoever imagined from his manner that he was simply indifferent made a sad mistake. He realized to the full the force of the blow that had fallen upon him, but he was made of the sort of metal that does not break under beating. His thoughts went out in the hour of his own stress to the unhappiness of many who, on the strength of his name, had bought electric stock at its price of two days before, and seen it drop forty per cent in twenty-four hours. He drew some consolation from the fact that the local stock exchange had closed its doors that morning, to remain shut till the storm blew over, and he issued statements to the newspapers advising all shareholders not to throw their holdings overboard in the panic but wait till the air cleared and the Company righted itself, as he was convinced it would soon. Conditions, he admitted, were not the same in 1891, because the Company had now exhausted its market for junior securities, and another solution than a fresh issue would have to be devised for the present difficulty.

The failure of the Electric and Manufacturing Company carried down with it for a short time three other Westinghouse concerns: the Machine Company, the Nernst Lamp Company — a minor personal venture of Westinghouse's — and the Security Investment Company. As the troubles of this trio were adjustable separately, they need not occupy our attention further; and neither the Air Brake Company nor the Union Switch and Signal Company was affected at all.

The creditors divided themselves naturally into

four groups, each of which appointed a committee to represent it in the negotiations which were to follow. That chosen by the bankers was the "reorganization" committee proper, and to coöperate with it there were a merchandise creditors' committee, an employees' committee, and a stockholders' committee. The bankers, representing clients in Pittsburgh, New York, Boston, Chicago, and a string of lesser cities and towns stretching from the Atlantic Coast to the Pacific, vetoed peremptorily most of the plans first proposed. The other committees seemed generally sympathetic with the desire of Westinghouse himself that measures be adopted for immediate relief, trusting to time and the obvious momentum of the Company's business to work out the ultimate salvation of all the interests concerned. The more conservative element among them looked less kindly upon his insistence that the support of the foreign companies and branches should be especially safeguarded in any agreement reached, for the objectors could see in these offspring only a drag upon the parent company.

Scheme after scheme was put forward only to be swept aside, and it was not till toward the end of March, 1908, that a basis was reached on which all parties could come together. Although the chief credit for it undoubtedly was due to Westinghouse, it came to be known as the merchandise creditors' plan, because it had for its central idea the funding of substantially the entire debt of the Company into stock, and this would demand of the merchandise creditors, as a matter of course, a heavier sacrifice than of any one else.   They were to accept four million dollars' worth of new stock in liquidation of their claims, and, as ten million dollars was fixed as the sum required to procure the dissolution of the receivership, the remaining six million dollars was to be obtained by offering that amount of new stock for subscription by the existing shareholders.   The banks were required, under the same plan, to merge half their claims in convertible five per cent bonds, and the remaining half either in stock at par, or in fifteen-year notes at the same rate of interest; with the option that the second half might be divided, three fifths going into five per cent notes maturing serially in four, five, and six years, and the other two fifths into stock at par.

The banks could as a rule see little virtue in this project; those that yielded most readily did so only on the assurance that if they did not take this they might lose more by a forced liquidation and the permanent ruin of the Company.   Some months later a number who had been holding out discovered that the new shares were already rising in market value, and consented to exchange their claims for the securities offered.   The stockholders were yet harder to deal with.   Many raised the objection that they had not the requisite money in hand; a larger number declared that the stock they already owned had plunged them into misfortune, and they did not wish any more of the same sort.   It was to the latter class that the stockholders' committee addressed itself most earnestly.

At first its letters were conciliatory in tone, expatiating on the duty of all shareholders to keep up a property of which they were the actual owners; these were followed by diplomatic suggestions that a general and ready response would capture public attention, stimulate the market for the securities, send up prices, and make a neat profit for those subscribers who came in at once. Still later came plain warnings that, unless the reorganization plan were soon put into operation, the bondholders would force a sale and the stock would be wholly wiped out, its holders recovering not a penny of the money they had spent on it. But, though the final date for closing the subscription list was postponed again and again, and "last call" followed "last call" with mortifying regularity; though the bankers, whose position was so strong that they could have wrecked everything by an inconsiderate move, had seen a new light; though Westinghouse personally took up a million and a half dollars of the new stock; though independent banking and brokerage houses which could have kept quite out of the atmosphere of trouble voluntarily opened their books for subscriptions and offered to advance the needed money to subscribers: about eighteen hundred of the four thousand stockholders were still, as late as October 1, 1908, refusing to take over their allotments of the new stock, and even November 20 found few of the laggards in line.

Against this showing stood forth in brilliant contrast the action of the Company's employees, most of them men whose limited means had been accumulated from their daily savings. In the first days of the reorganization agitation, being recognized as parties in interest because their livelihood was temporarily at stake on the survival of the business, they had appointed a committee to canvass among their own body for subscriptions to the new stock. When, at the general conference, the work to be accomplished was apportioned among the several committees, the volume of subscriptions assigned to the employees' committee to collect was three hundred ninety-five thousand, six hundred fifty dollars; on the final day of reckoning, it came forward with six hundred eleven thousand, two hundred fifty dollars, collected from about five thousand of the workers — a striking exhibition of loyalty and intelligence on the part of the men who knew at first hand what was actually going on in the shops.

On December 5, 1908, less than fourteen months after the appointment of the receivers, the Company was taken out of their hands and restored to the stockholders, purged of most of the immediate ills which had beset it. Its net debt had been reduced from more than forty-four million dollars to less than thirty-one million dollars, and its annual interest burden by one million dollars; while its capital stock, on which there was no fixed liability, had been increased from twenty-nine million dollars to forty-one million dollars, all sorts of floating debts having been merged in this increase. There was also another and radical change, of which Westinghouse had received intimations but of which he had not realized the imminence. In pursuance of an arrangement entered into when the reorganization plan was adopted, the

bankers and merchandise creditors who had undertaken to put it through took control of the administration and elected a new board of sixteen directors,
selected mainly from among the members of the several committees. This board chose for its chairman
Robert Mather, a lawyer of a conservative bent of
mind, who had had large experience in the management of the Rock Island Railway. Westinghouse
was left in the office of president, but his authority
was limited to the operating and sales departments,
and the direction of all financial affairs was vested
in Mather.

Temperamentally the two men were wholly un-
congenial. The boundary line between their respective fields was sometimes indistinct in spite of
every effort to define it; both men were very positive
in their mental attitude toward any question presented which offered a possibility for difference: and
the difficulty of the situation was intensified by the
fact that Westinghouse had been for so many years
not only the titular head of the Company but its
practical dictator. The result was not hard to fore-
see, especially as unfortunate outside conditions
made the first year meager in profits. In January,
1910, the directors adopted what on its face seemed
a highly complimentary resolution, granting Westinghouse a six months' leave of absence. Soon reports
gained circulation, however, that the vacation he
was invited to take was merely a subterfuge to cover
a quarrel between him and the chairman of the board,
which, as the directors sided with their chairman,
pointed to the early retirement of the president.

These stories proved only too true. At the annual meeting in July, Westinghouse did not appear or make any effort for reëlection, and the directors elected Edwin F. Atkins, a prominent manufacturer and merchant of Boston, to the presidency. By the summer of 1911, the Company having in the interval taken sundry courses which he believed unprogressive and injurious, Westinghouse was ready to open a campaign for reinstatement, but later reconsidered this purpose. Nevertheless, when he entered the annual meeting he carried in his pocket proxies which, with his own holding, represented about two hundred thousand shares. His endeavor to make these effective by moving to permit cumulative voting was defeated by the majority in control, who swung four hundred and ninety thousand votes for any measure or candidate they favored.

This was the last appearance of Westinghouse as a conspicuous figure in the Electric and Manufacturing Company which he founded and had conducted for the better part of twenty years, and which, of all his many enterprises, held the supreme place in his heart. With his elimination ends the story of the rehabilitation of his corporation after a fall which an eminent economist has described as "in point of size, the most considerable mercantile failure America has ever witnessed." [1] Tragic as the finale was, not a dissenting note was audible in the comments it drew forth from thoughtful men all over the world, dwelling upon the enormous debt of gratitude

[1] "Corporate Promotions and Reorganizations," by Arthur S. Dewing, Ph. D.

that humanity owed George Westinghouse **for** what he had accomplished as a fearless captain of industry, even though a combination of untoward circumstances had prevented his reaping the full measure **of m**aterial reward he had so richly earned.

CHAPTER XVI

AIR SPRINGS AND ADDRESSES

AFTER George Westinghouse had been forced out of the presidency of his Electric and Manufacturing Company, his old friends recalled a remark he made to the group of Pittsburgh bankers who, in 1891, refused to lend him the sum he needed in an emergency: "Well, gentlemen, this only compels me to do something else." He had no notion of being laid upon the shelf. His Machine Company was busy making gas engines and turbines, and to the development of these he devoted himself with the zeal of an artist coming back with a fresh eye to a half-finished picture. Beside the mechanisms to which he had already given attention in the past, he found a new one to interest him, and he owed the discovery, as he had so many of its predecessors, to an accident.

The first use of automobiles in this country gave scant promise of their present universality. Their cost, their load limitations, their liability to get out of order, and their general untrustworthiness for long pulls, at that time, led most practical observers to discredit the idea of their ever superseding the delivery dray, the street car, or the suburban railway for everyday transportation. In view of his almost lifelong association with the railroad industry, it is hardly wonderful that the usually progressive Westinghouse was among the ultra-conservatives on this point. If he wished to go somewhere for a definite purpose, he was glad to go by the shortest route and the most expeditious conveyance, but rushing through the air for the mere sake of rest and refreshment had no attractions for him; and when finally, in 1904, he was induced to let the French Westinghouse Works build an elaborately equipped limousine car for him as an exhibit of workmanship, his surrender to a business argument involved no change in his personal prejudices. In the last years of his life, it may be said in passing, he became a convert to the utilitarian view of the automobile, and used one constantly in running between Pittsburgh and the little towns in Turtle Creek Valley where his various shops were situated.

It was while he was still unconverted to the new mode of locomotion and ready to consider any fact to its disparagement, that he accompanied Mrs. Westinghouse one day on a trip in their limousine from Lenox, Massachusetts, to Kingston, New York. The chauffeur happened to overlook an obscure but deep depression in the road, the car plunged into it, and with the rebound of the springs the passengers were thrown violently out of their seats, Westinghouse striking his head against the roof with a force which would have wounded him seriously had not his straw hat served for a buffer. As he removed the ruined headgear and looked ruefully at it, his first thought appears to have been not so much of rebuking the chauffeur as of condemning a machine which was capable of giving its occupants such an experience. What were inflated rubber tires for, if not to break the jars on a rough road? And of what use were the best of steel springs, unless they would prevent one from being racked to pieces between holes and hummocks? Possibly not much could be done to improve the action of the tires, but might it not be possible to make the springs more efficient? To this question he addressed himself with pencil and drawing-board immediately on reaching Lenox again. His sketches he carried later to Pittsburgh and had a model pair of springs constructed, which he brought to Lenox and tested on the limousine. When he had tinkered with these long enough to locate their chief shortcomings, he made another pair; and thus, swinging between Pittsburgh and Lenox, he kept up his alterations and experiments till he chanced one day to mention the matter to an old friend, who asked him whether he had ever heard of a spring invented by a mechanic in Watervliet, New York.

"No," he answered. "What kind of a spring?"

"Compressed air."

There was magic in the words. The memory of his old successes came back to him with a thrill, and with no unnecessary delay he visited Watervliet and hunted up the inventor, who proved to be a German machinist named Richard Liebau. Looking over the model, it did not take Westinghouse long to see where its defects lay.

"You have a valuable invention here," he commented with characteristic frankness, "but it is crude in some details. For one thing, it leaks."

Liebau admitted that the fault was a bad one, but added that neither he nor the friends who had worked with him had been able to hit upon any satisfactory remedy for it, though they had tried many devices.

"Come with me to Pittsburgh," said Westinghouse, "and we'll study it out together." And that was what they did.

The Liebau device was of elemental simplicity in arrangement, consisting of four air cushions located between the body of the car and the axles, one at each corner. The cushions were metal cylinders, with pistons working in them so that the confined air acted as a spring, the most resilient medium available. The particular method by which the leakage was cured was the invention of Westinghouse; and though to the final development of the air spring as we know it to-day there were important contributions by the engineering force to whom the matter was delegated, the determining factor was supplied by the head of the house. In his earlier experiments, he had great hope of being able to dispense with the use of pneumatic tires, and with this end in view he fitted two or three cars with air springs and solid tires of various forms, and also invented and constructed spring wheels; but though, as was his usual habit in such matters, he dealt with the subject broadly and attacked it from every point of view, he finally became convinced that for fast-running pleasure cars there had not yet been devised any substitute for pneumatic tires.

A company was formed for the manufacture of the air spring, and it derives a pathetic interest from the fact that it is the last considerable undertaking of the kind in which the great inventor ever engaged. It proved to be a profitable enterprise, and since his death his son, the present George Westinghouse, has been its president.

It was only after his release from the heaviest of his executive responsibilities that Westinghouse may be said to have found himself as a public speaker. During the most active years of his busy life he had been called upon from time to time to make an after-dinner speech at a gathering of his associates, or offer a few words of welcome when a party of foreign visitors were to be entertained. We have seen how he dreaded facing an audience with even the most informal of utterances, and he discredited every assurance given him by his, hearers that he had acquitted himself well and needed only a little more assurance to do better yet. One virtue of his speeches lay in their always dealing with some subject with which he was thoroughly familiar, and, thanks to his lack of artificial training, he expounded his views with a directness that atoned for any inelegances of expression. These facts alone would have sufficed to account for the frequency of the demands made upon him now that he was supposed to have more leisure than of old; but another factor of quite as much importance was the widespread desire among his professional colleagues to prove that, whatever estimate the commercial world might put upon his work as a financier, their admiration of him as an engineer and their affection for him as a man had suffered no diminution. On every occasion which would afford them a pretext, therefore, they called upon him for an address, and to not a few calls he responded. His themes were happily chosen to fit the situation and the times, and his treatment of them was appropriately practical.

His installation as president of the American Society of Mechanical Engineers occurred soon after the Taft administration had begun its sweeping war upon alleged offenders against the antitrust law ; and the kernel of his address on taking the chair was a declaration that "there never was a time in the history of the world when honest, wise, and conservative action is more strongly demanded of us and of all men than now, if we have any desire to preserve the right to carry on comfortably our various affairs."

At a dinner of the American Engineering Societies held the following year in Boston, he expanded this point. "For many years," said he, "the tendencies have been strongly toward large and powerful railway and industrial combinations. Their very magnitude, coupled with the evil practices so frequently disclosed in the press and in our law courts, has so aroused the public that there is now a fixed determination to establish by national and State laws an exacting governmental control of practically all forms of corporations, in order that competition may be encouraged and not stifled, but seemingly with due regard to the real objects in view — the securing of the best public service in all forms, the best foods and goods for our daily needs, the greatest possible comfort to the masses, and as great freedom as possible from those restrictions which hinder rather than promote honest endeavor. Many of the hardships which will arise might have been avoided by those responsible for the creation of great combinations had they appreciated the inevitable consequences of their selfish and unwise course in suppressing competition by methods transparently wrong. But fortunately there are indications that the great leaders are alive to the importance of the regulation of legislation, and the creation of a sentiment which will bring business men to their senses. The engineering societies, by joint action, have it in their power to do much. Probably there is no better way than to show, from their knowledge and experience, that unregulated competition and rivalry in business have made our costs greater and rendered ideal conditions in industrial and engineering matters most difficult of realization.

"I need only call your attention to the effects of this unregulated competition in one great industry — the electrical — which has grown up in less than twenty-five years. No user of electrical apparatus can fail to appreciate the advantage it would be to him, when some repair part is needed, if certain standards were followed by all constructors with reference to equivalent devices; but it is lamentable to say that with the single exception of uniform bases for incandescent lamps, there are now practically no standards. The vast majority of our inventors proceed along independent lines, with the result of a constantly growing confusion, to the disadvantage of everybody."

By way of illustrating the evils of this unsystematic mode of proceeding, the speaker cited the case of one large electrical company which manufactured a standard motor, yet whose customers were continually requesting estimates on special motors embracing some particular feature of a motor made by another manufacturer. These special estimates, even on motors of less than two-hundred horse power, amounted in a single year to about ten thousand in number, involving departures from the standard motor in horse power or speed rating, or dimensions of base, or dimensions over all, or height from base to center of shaft, or weight, or method of lubrication, or size of shaft, or guaranty of performance. Such demands, of course, laid a heavy burden upon the manufacturer, and inconvenienced the purchaser by increased expense and delayed deliveries; and the experience of the company alluded to was paralleled by that of fifty others, every one of which had its individual patterns and designs, so that probably fifty thousand needless variations in motors alone had required an addition of many millions of dollars to the investment already made in installations of electrical machinery.

The speaker ended with a plea for coöperation among electrical engineers and manufacturers by some means like an interchange of products and a system of license agreements enabling one to obtain the use of another's patents on the payment of a royalty. And in order to establish a mutual working basis equally fair to all, he believed that the parties in interest, instead of calling for more Government regulation, might better organize a well-equipped and officered bureau of standardization and maintain it at their joint expense.

The same central idea animated several other speeches made during the same period. Coöperation and standardization seemed to Westinghouse the crying needs of the hour in all industries, in view of their saving of waste in money, thought, and effort. In an address prepared for delivery at the meeting of the American Society of Mechanical Engineers with the Institution of Mechanical Engineers in London in the summer of 1910, he took for his subject "The Electrification of Railways", and devoted himself to showing the imperative need for the selection of one electric system for universal use. Referring to the ambition once cherished by certain railway managers to individualize their roads by adopting for them gauges which would prevent the cars and locomotives of connecting lines from trespassing on their tracks, he recalled the fact that, as lately as 1878, there were in the United States eleven different gauges beside the standard gauge of 4 feet 8½ inches adopted by Stephenson and since become general. When the necessity for unification came to be recognized, the cost of changing gauges was very burdensome to the roads which had it to do, in some instances fastening a permanent debt upon them. He laid down as five fundamental requisites for standardizing steam lines: a standard gauge of track, a standard of interchangeable type of coupling for vehicles, a uniform interchangeable type of brake apparatus, interchangeable heat apparatus, and a uniform system of train signals. To these must be added, in the case of electric railways, three more: a supply of electricity of uniform quality as to voltage and periodicity; conductors for this, so uniformly placed with reference to the rails that, without change of any kind, an electrically-fitted locomotive or car can collect its supply of current when on the lines of other companies; and uniform apparatus for control of electric supply, whereby two or more electrically-fitted locomotives or cars from different lines can be operated together from one locomotive or car.

His repeated prophecy of the ultimate electrification of all the great railways remains still unfulfilled, but many transportation experts who scoffed at the notion when he first broached it afterward admitted to him that the change would be only a question of time. In the light of this, it seemed to him all important that the choice of the uniform system should be made without more delay. Railway electrification, he argued, had so far been limited to small areas, usually where the unsuitableness of steam locomotives for tunnel and terminal service had compelled the substitution of electric motors there; but these limited zones were expanding and after a time would meet; and then the same conditions which had compelled the adoption of certain common standards for the steam railways would apply still more forcibly to the electric railways, and the cost of altering everything over would be a very serious matter.

Another favorite line followed by Westinghouse in his prophecies had to do with the progressively increasing use of electricity in quarters where at first it had been slow in making its way. This was the burden of his speech to the Southern Commercial Congress at Atlanta in the spring of 1911. The South, said he, was abundantly blessed with coal mines and waterfalls, and from these resources could be drawn the vital forces of industry and transportation. The magic agent which would take the energy of the South's hidden coal, her air, and her falling water, carry it by easy channels, and cause it to give the light of a million candles and the power of a thousand men, move great loads faster than horses can travel, produce heat without combustion, and unlock chemical bonds and release new materials, was electricity. The water courses in the Appalachian Mountains could be made to develop from five to seven million horse power during the dry seasons of the year and a much larger quantity at other times. By the use of the alternating current, enough power could be taken from a single dynamo for operating telephone and telegraph lines, for producing light and heat, for running street cars and railway trains, for working mines and mills and factories, and for electrochemical operations. As it was possible to transmit power hundreds of miles from its source, water courses unavailable for other uses because of their inaccessibility or unwholesome surroundings could be made to furnish power to distant cities, and run factories planted on high and healthful sites, or on the outskirts of any town where labor is most plentiful and transportation facilities are best. He mentioned one power company in the South which at that time was drawing power from a number of different streams in different States, and lighting forty-five cities and towns, and furnishing current for six street-railway systems, besides keeping hundreds of motors at work for miscellaneous purposes.

Lines of industry which could be successfully developed in the South by electric power, he added, were gold, copper, iron, and coal mining; ore reduction; food canning; manufacturing textiles, cement, fertilizers, lumber, furniture, paper, shoes and leather, and agricultural implements; iron and steel making; road building, and oil refining. Moreover, experiments made by Sir Oliver Lodge indicated that the electric stimulation of plant growth might yet be made to produce wonderful results.

This was his last notable public address, and its concluding passages are significant for their revelation of the backward and forward movements of his mind. His painful memories of the close of his connection with his Electric and Manufacturing Company were reflected in an earnest plea for cumulative voting in the government of corporations, as a protection for the minority stockholders against the machinations of a majority clique. The final sentence of all has a most interesting ring in these

days when militarism and preparedness are upper-
most topics of popular discussion.   Impressing upon
young men the importance of learning the lessons
of self-restraint and obedience to authority, and
drawing for illustration upon the value of his own
experiences as a soldier, he said: "The present
preëminence of Germany in industrial matters arises
very largely from the military training and discipline
to which each of her citizens must submit."

CHAPTER XVII

A Big Man's Human Side

An evening I shall always remember was passed in Pittsburgh late in January, 1916. The occasion was an annual dinner of the Veteran Employees' Association of the Westinghouse Electric and Manufacturing Company, to whose membership those persons are eligible who have been in the Company's employ for twenty years or longer. Several hundred diners, including a small group of guests at the speakers' table, sat down together, and a more impressive gathering I never attended. The strong, intelligent, and interested faces, the manly and mutually courteous bearing of these men of the bench and the machine shop, conveyed the finest of lessons in true American democracy; and the speeches which followed the clearing of the tables told a yet more eloquent story, for they explained what had held this body of workers at their posts so many years in an era of fitful change. Every speaker had his contribution, large or small, to add to the common fund of reminiscence, and every story had for its central figure one powerful personality; and the acme was reached when, with an appropriate introduction, the curtain which concealed a large object hanging against the wall in the rear of the hall was drawn aside, and revealed a square bronze relief portrait of the hero of the evening, George Westinghouse.

It was the work of the eminent sculptor, Lorado Taft, and contributed by the Association as a gift from its members to the Company they had served so long, to be hung in the main passageway of the mammoth building at East Pittsburgh, where every one could see it daily in going to and from his work. It represented the founder in the attitude he always preferred in the rare instances when he had consented to pose for a picture: seated in an armchair, his hands grasping the arms, his face full to the front, and his eyes aimed straight into those of his vis-à-vis, as if he had paused only for the moment in passing, and was preparing to rise and move on again as soon as released. It was the George Westinghouse of rapid action whom they all knew in life — earnest, tense, direct, aggressive, willful, forward-looking, regardless of obstacles, contemptuous of leisure, unsparing of self. Nature had written in that face the faults as well as the virtues of the soul behind it. The speeches of the evening had been equally impartial in their reflection of both. It was an experience meeting, not a mere council of eulogy. But when the whims and foibles, the eccentricities and inconsistencies of the lost leader were touched upon, it was always in the genial spirit of real affection, and the balance cast between his triumphs and his failures left nothing to be desired by his best lover. A finer tribute of loyalty to one who was no longer where he could respond to it is impossible to imagine.

Nor was this sentiment reserved simply for public display. Wherever I have gone among the officers and men of the Westinghouse companies, I have found the same attitude toward their late chief on the part of those who ever came into personal contact with him, no matter how slightly; and the air of Pittsburgh is surcharged today with Westinghouse legends and traditions, of which I cannot attempt to give more than a passing hint.

Though modest and simple in manner, and friendly in his mode of approach to even the humblest of his employees, able to call a multitude of them by their given names, and everywhere known among them as "the Boss" or "the Old Man", not one would have ventured upon an unbecoming familiarity with him. Nature had stamped him with a dignity which made even the suggestion of such a thing impossible; yet there was not a man who was afraid to come to him frankly when there was something that needed saying. It might be to meet a rebuff at the outset, but justice was sure to come later.

Tucked in among the works at East Pittsburgh stood for some years an unpretentious den known as "the Old Man's shop." To it Westinghouse would repair when he came to the Works with an idea in mind to which he wished to give his undivided attention for a while. Thirty or forty mechanics and draftsmen were within speaking distance, ready at his call to drop whatever they were at and proceed to the development of his latest conceit. It made no difference where he was — in New York or Washington, or up in the Berkshire Hills, or traveling in his "movie home", the private car, Glen Eyre — his secretary was at his elbow; and when a thought of apparent value occurred to him, he either dictated an outline of it, or sat down and made a sketch to mail to his experimental laboratory from that next stopping-place, preceding this if possible with full instructions by long-distance telephone, directly to the foreman whom he intrusted with the translation of the theory into solid metal. Many amusing stories are told of this habit. "If Mr. Westinghouse," said one of his foremen the other day, "telephoned that a certain minor part was to be one sixteenth of an inch in diameter, and on his arrival he found it one eighth of an inch, he would send for the man responsible for tampering with his orders, and demand his reasons. If they were insufficient, the man received on the spot some candid admonitions about doing what he was told, and later perhaps a bit of discipline; but if he made out a good case by showing that his change was wise, he was equally likely to be marked for promotion."

A tireless and rapid worker himself, Westinghouse found it difficult to understand any different habit on the part of a subordinate. He was chary of direct praise, and sometimes when a man had accomplished what would generally be considered a wonderful feat, he would show no appreciation of the effort. One day he sent a hurry order of some magnitude to a foreman who, anxious to make a record, set to work at it instantly with a gang of picked men. For two days and two nights they labored without rest and almost without food.

Westinghouse turned up before the job was quite complete and wanted to know how far they had got with it. The foreman, with a thrill of pride, showed him the almost finished machine. His only comment was a whimsical: "Is *that* all you've done!"

In spite of this outward attitude, he was inwardly most appreciative of faithful and efficient service. To others than the man immediately concerned, he was generous in awarding commendation where deserved, and his habit in this respect was felt by some of his older associates to have been overdone in favor of certain newcomers in his organizations before there had been a real test of their merits.

Of a skilled mechanician who was one of his mainstays for years, he once demanded:

"Miller, why are you always so slow about getting out any job I order? Why can't you be quick as Herr is?"

And of Mr. Herr, the next time they met · "Herr, why on earth can't you take example from Miller, and do things promptly?"

Soon afterward, the two men chanced to come together on something, and Miller asked:

"What is it you have been doing for the Boss, Mr. Herr, that makes him always tell me how much quicker you are in your work than I am?"

"Why, Miller," answered Herr, "that was the very question I was going to put to *you!*"

On one occasion Herr got the better of these speeding-up methods, but with a highly characteristic sequel. He had just come home from a business trip and found awaiting him a message from his chief, who also had been out of town, telling him to have a certain casting made which was needed for immediate use at the Switch and Signal shops. It was Saturday night, but Herr lost no time in opening communication with one of the foremen at the Air-Brake Works and asking him whether he could not call a few men together and put this job through. The foreman did so, and bright and early on Sunday morning Herr hastened to join them at the Works.

"Sam," he inquired, "how far along have you got with that casting?"

"It's done," answered the foreman, "but it's mighty hot still."

"Never mind that. Have you a team that you can hitch up at once?"

"Yes, sir."

"Then carry the casting down to the Switch and Signal shops."

The foreman obeyed. A few minutes later Westinghouse appeared.

"Herr," said he, "did you get my message?"

"I did."

"When are you going to pour that casting?"

"It's poured already."

"Ha! How soon can you get it out?"

"It's out."

"Is that so? Where is it?"

"At the Switch and Signal shop."

The speechlessness with which Westinghouse was smitten for perhaps two seconds, betrayed the depth of his astonishment; but as usual he expressed no surprise, and bolting forthwith for the road, he called back over his shoulder:

"Well, I'll go right down there myself and hustle those fellows up!"

Among his other strictly human traits, Westinghouse would occasionally act on first impulse, and not with the wisdom which is born of careful consideration. He was, however, quite as quick to repent as to act, when he saw he was in error. A foreman who, though they had always been the best of friends, happened to cross his path in one of his impulsive moments, received a severe rating for having failed to perform some practical impossibility. The rebuke itself was hard enough to bear, but might have been overlooked if it had not been hurled at the man in the presence of a number of his underlings — a circumstance which was liable, in his judgment, to be fatal to his authority. He sought his employer a few minutes later, and began, with respect in his manner but repressed wrath in his voice:

"I think the time has come, Mr. Westinghouse, when we must part company. I can't rest quiet under such humiliation as you put upon me this morning. I am not obliged to, and I won't!"

Westinghouse looked up from his writing with an air of good-humored deprecation.

"Oh, come now!" he pleaded. "Remember that I am only human. When things go wrong, I am apt to blow off my feelings at the first person that gets in the way. The next time you see that I am in a bad temper, just hurry out of my reach. If I try to follow you up, don't pay any attention to me, but keep right on."

Another foreman who usually was noted for minding his own business came to Westinghouse one day and stated his suspicions, with the specific facts which had aroused them, that certain officers of one of his companies in whom Westinghouse had till then felt the utmost confidence, were engaged in systematic graft. Westinghouse indignantly refused to listen to the charges, and his informant went away with a sense of having blundered, and given offense rather than assistance to the chief. Not very long thereafter, Westinghouse himself stumbled upon proofs which left him no alternative but to realize the truth, and he promptly dismissed the guilty men from office. Afterward he sought the loyal foreman and reproached him for not having insisted at first upon making the case clear.

"But, Mr. Westinghouse," protested the man, "I said all I could, and you wouldn't listen to me."

"Why on earth didn't you *make* me listen?" exclaimed Westinghouse, and then laughed in spite of himself.

Coming into the Machine Works one morning with a bundle of papers in his hand, Westinghouse summoned Miller to his workroom. He had thought out something new on a line with which his mind had been busy since childhood, the invention of a perfect rotary engine. The present scheme was more elaborate than anything he had ever proposed before, involving an extraordinary internal arrangement with fans and other unusual accessories. At his request Miller gave a thorough examination to the drawings and specifications for the new device.

"I want a model made like that," said the inventor.

"Do you realize what you are ordering, Mr. Westinghouse?" asked Miller. "It will cost a small fortune to build such a model."

"Never mind, I want it done."

"But the thing won't work in any event as you expect it to."

"I know what I want. Go ahead and make it."

Accordingly the model was made, at a large expense. It did not take Westinghouse ten minutes to see that Miller's warning of its uselessness had been correct.

"Mr. Westinghouse," said Miller, "I hated to see you throw your money into the ditch like that."

"Oh," answered Westinghouse cheerfully, "it wasn't thrown away. Think how many men it kept employed; and besides, it is one more step toward ultimate success."

As has been indicated, Westinghouse was a strong believer in the virtue of having his own way. He had no liking for advice; he preferred to follow his instincts and issue his commands accordingly. There were a certain few men, however, who had made a mark in the world for their brilliancy of achievement on whose simple dicta he was sometimes ready to hazard a large stake. One of these, an English physicist of great renown, had demonstrated, through the process of reasoning, that the extraction of heat from the atmosphere for the purpose of developing power was a theoretical possibility, and had in a general way indicated the method and type of machines that would be required in the process. He, however, stated that this apparatus would have to be so cumbersome and expensive as to make the scheme of no practical value. Westinghouse accepted the scientific basis as sound, but disagreed with respect to the impossibility of reducing it to practice. A comprehensive series of futile experiments, during which many ingenious devices were developed and constructed, compelled him to admit reluctantly that it was a tougher problem than he had anticipated, and he finally conceded that his scientific friend was right, in both premises and conclusions.

Westinghouse was so expert a practical mechanic that when he laid his hand actually to a bit of construction the men who worked near him used to say with a chuckle· "The Boss is on the job; all we have to do is to pass him the tools." In the drafting rooms he had a trick of dropping down at any time in front of a desk and busying himself with whatever drawings lay on its surface. Sometimes he would reach out his right hand, and, without lifting his eyes from the paper before him, utter the single word· "Pencil!" The draftsman next him would place a pencil in the outstretched fingers, and with this he would amend the drawing in some particular or outline a new one very rapidly, pausing only when he discovered that he had made a mark which he had better change. Then, still without the slightest diversion of the eyes, out would come the hand again, and with it the single word: "Rubber!" Into the hand would go the rubber as the pencil had gone a moment earlier, and he would erase the rejected line, brush away the dust with his little finger, and resume drawing in a silence as profound as before.

It was a standing joke among his lieutenants that they never could guess "where the Old Man was going to break out next." One who was attending to some business in Denver suddenly received, out of a clear sky, a telegram ordering him to go to Idaho and hunt up a certain person, and referring him, by way of explanation, to an article published in the latest issue of a well-known weekly newspaper. This proved to be a story about a wonderful agricultural discovery recently made. An Idaho farmer, it said, having gone to the Yukon country on a hunt for gold, had accidentally stumbled there upon a field of wheat which, for height of stalk and fullness of head, excelled anything he had ever seen or heard of. He carried away some of it, and, after his return to Idaho, planted the kernels; their yield the next season was most abundant, and absolutely true to type. His discovery, the story concluded, had caused great excitement among the Northwestern farmers, who were flocking to his ranch and buying seed of him at one dollar a pound.

The recipient of the telegram went to Idaho at once, hunted up the man, and found him, as described, doing a thriving business. Later communications from Westinghouse revealed the fact that he had happened to read the article, and been suddenly struck with a fancy for buying the farmer's entire stock of seed, to use for the rapid replenishment of the American wheat supply. His idea was that this might aid to solve one of the food problems of our poor by making it possible presently to reduce the price of bread.

All who have worked under him agree as to the marvelous gift he had for inspiring his subordinates. This was due not only to his personal magnetism, but to his habit of giving every one a chance. He used to take heavy contracts for things that would need a large amount of development work, and then call upon his experts to turn them out; and every man knew what it would mean to make a success of the task. Indeed, the reason Westinghouse was always in the lead among the inventors of his generation was that he commanded the talents and the best efforts of many able young men to supplement his own. Toward the group upon whom he specially leaned he had as strong a sense of loyalty as they had toward him. At times when the money market was tight he was obliged to limit their cash salaries to dimensions which he frankly said were insufficient, but he would make it up to them by generous gifts of stock.

He had a large way of doing everything. Frank H. Taylor, who in February, 1902, was promoted to be second vice-president of the Electric & Manufacturing Company, preserves, as if it were a patent of nobility, a very short letter he received at that time from Westinghouse, stating what would be expected of him. "The duties of the second vice-president," ran the letter —

"will be general, comprehending the important contract relations of the company, the sale of the company's products, and general supervision of the company's properties and operations, wherever situated. He will also assume final responsibility, subject to the president, for the conduct of the general offices, and the purchasing, store and cost departments; he will advise with the other officers with respect to the duties assigned to them, and will participate in and preside at the meetings of the heads of the various branches of the company's business."

"Here," said Mr. Taylor, in showing me the letter, "are ten lines of typewriting, clearly turning over to my management a property of, say, sixty million dollars in value — an example of simplicity and directness of thought and expression which it would be hard to match."

Nikola Tesla, who perfected his inventions in alternating-current apparatus while associated with George Westinghouse and receiving his financial support, once publicly paid his patron this cordial tribute · "He is one of those few men who conscientiously respect intellectual property, and who acquire their right to use inventions by fair and equitable means. . . . Had other industrial firms and manufacturers been as just and liberal as Mr. Westinghouse, I should have had many more of my inventions in use than I now have."

The same sort of testimony is heard wherever

one goes. Hugh Rodman, for instance, founder and head of the Rodman Chemical Company of East Pittsburgh, described to me his experience in these words:

"For several years I was research engineer for the Machine Company, making such investigations as Mr. Westinghouse or the management directed, and, as a matter of course, turning over the results to the company. One investigation carried me to the case-hardening department, where, after considerable work, I developed patentable processes and materials which apparently had commercial value apart from the company's ordinary activities. These I reported as usual, and the question was raised as to who properly owned them. I held that, as the company was not interested in chemical manufacturing, it should retain only a working right to the processes, leaving me to patent them for my own benefit in other respects. The company argued that, its money and equipment having been used, the processes belonged to it. We appealed to Mr. Westinghouse as arbitrator. His decision was that, though the company might legally maintain its right to the inventions, he would make no move to do so, and he not only turned over to me the entire rights in the inventions, but offered me enough capital to erect and run a small factory, of which he left me in full control. I feel great satisfaction in adding that the investment proved worth while, and in bearing this witness to his fine generosity!"

CHAPTER XVIII

"The Old Man" and His Employees

WHEN George Westinghouse established himself in business as a manufacturer of air brakes, in February, 1870, he had a rather primitive establishment. The first mechanic he hired was Christopher Horrocks, who at this writing is still in active service at the Air Brake Works in Wilmerding, as keenly interested in his duties and as full of enthusiasm as he ever was. When he came in, the factory was near the corner of Liberty Avenue and Twenty-fifth Street, in a building of which the main walls are standing today; it was then, he says, unfinished, the brickwork being up but neither window-framing nor doors being in place. The equipment consisted of "a steam engine about the size of a kitchen chair, a boiler two sheets in length, and a section of shafting." One man — Ralph Baggaley, whose acquaintance we have already made — constituted the entire office force; another, named Welsh, combined the functions of time-keeper, foreman, and superintendent; and Horrocks was the "horny-fisted son of toil" who did the work requiring brawn and muscle.

By degrees other men were brought in, till the shop began to assume a very busy air. Young Westinghouse was so approachable and pleasant-mannered as to command the most cordial liking from his little staff.   He also introduced several innovations which naturally heightened this feeling.   After his return from his first visit to England, for instance, he announced that work would be suspended every Saturday at noon, so that the men could have a half-holiday to enjoy as they pleased without trespassing upon their Sunday rest.   It was the first move of that kind that had ever been made in Pittsburgh, and, so far as known, in the United States, and it proved not only popular but in a larger sense profitable, for it gave the new shop a unique distinction among the local industries.   Meanwhile, in the autumn of the first year, he had invited the entire force, by that time embracing fifteen men, to dine with him at one of the city hotels on Thanksgiving day.   The dinner was in the interest of sociability and mutual understanding, and was repeated annually till it became impracticable on account of increasing numbers; as a substitute, the practice was adopted of presenting every employee, great or small, with a turkey to crown his Thanksgiving dinner with his family.

This custom continued for more than thirty years; but the pay roll meanwhile had swelled steadily till the fowls to be given away exceeded a dozen tons in weight, and were brought to the distributing point in big refrigerator cars.   Also, there had become connected with the Works not merely the generation they started with, but its successor; and, on the per capita basis of allotment, several turkeys were liable to find their way into a single family, while another, perhaps larger, would get only one.   A certain father, for example, had seven unmarried sons working with him in the Air Brake shops, and to that household went eight turkeys, though only one or two could be put to beneficial use. From such lavishness sprang up a habit, in large families, of resorting to some device like a shooting-match, a raffle, or a game of cards, for disposing of their surplus poultry. At the suggestion of John F. Miller, then secretary of the Company but now its president, Mr. Westinghouse decided to call a halt on what was becoming a serious abuse, and to substitute for it a pension system, for which the ten thousand dollars or thereabout that had been annually spent on turkeys, if suitably capitalized, would make a very comfortable nucleus. The principal sum thus evolved, amounting to one hundred and ten thousand dollars, was set aside and so invested as to produce a regular annual income, from which were paid pensions, ranging from twenty to one hundred dollars a month, to all employees who had rendered long and faithful service and become disabled, or reached the age of retirement — voluntary at sixty-five years, or compulsory at seventy. The widows, children, and other dependent relatives of the pensioners were placed on the roll at rates that varied according to specified conditions. The company made itself responsible for the pension fund and for any deficiencies of income that might occur.

Prior to the introduction of the pension system, there was established a relief department, which, though the company assumed the cost of foundation and maintenance, and held the principal fund in trust and paid interest on it, was relieved of all taint of gratuity by a roll of supporting membership, like a mutual insurance association.   Both fees and benefits were graded according to the wages or salaries of the members, and varied from a fee of fifty cents a month, earning benefits of $5 a week for a disabled member, to a monthly fee of $1.50 with a weekly benefit of $15; and on the death of any member, of whatever class, $150 was paid to his heirs.   Medical examinations were made, and attendance in case of accident furnished, free of charge to the members, by a physician or surgeon at the headquarters of the department.   These advantages were later duplicated in the main by the Electric and Manufacturing Company, but the Air Brake Company has enlarged and liberalized them by degrees till in many respects they are today unique in the industrial world.

At all the Westinghouse works, the ideal kept constantly in view was coöperation.   The desire of the founder, as manifested in such ways as I have just been describing, was to have every person connected with one of his companies, whether as officer, agent, or employee, feel that he was part of the concern, that its interests were his interests, and that its personnel was one big family.   To that end every proper encouragement was given to the workmen to organize clubs and societies among themselves for the promotion of good fellowship and the perpetuation of the memories of old times.   The effect of such a policy shows itself in the pride with which the older men in the works refer to their long connection with their Company, much as so many veteran

servants of the Government point to the stars and
chevrons they wear. It was in pursuance of this
coöperative ideal not less than for the moral and
physical good to be derived from them, that the
Westinghouse companies have spent large sums on
Christian Association and Welfare buildings, and
presented them to the communities adjacent to their
works, so that the employees and their families could
have facilities for wholesome recreation out of
working hours.

Another ambition entertained by George Westinghouse was to educate his own people, as far as practicable, for their duties under him, instead of leaving
them to pick up their technical instruction haphazard. More has been done in this direction by
the Electric and Manufacturing Company and the
Machine Company than by any other of the Westinghouse corporations — doubtless because the work
there required more systematically trained faculties.
In East Pittsburgh is maintained a technical night
school which offers, at a nominal expense, a very
good drill in the fundamentals of mathematics, engineering, shop practice, and mechanical work, to
any youth who is unable to study in the daytime;
the boys who attend it fraternize like members of a
college class, and get a great deal of social enjoyment
as well as mental stimulation out of their connection
with it. The Machine Company supports an ap-
prenticeship course for male pupils sixteen years of
age or older. The apprentices are required to sign
articles for a certain number of years, are paid at a
modest rate for every hour they work, and at the

close of a successful course receive a present of $100. Mr. C. R. Dooley, an alumnus of a Western university, with a technical education and a strong bent for teaching and social enterprises, makes an annual tour of the colleges of the country, picking up members of their graduating classes who have a taste for some line of engineering, and who seem to offer promising material for the Westinghouse working corps. If they are taken on, he keeps in close touch with them through the medium of a young men's club of which he is an active manager.

Nor are the girls in the works overlooked in the general welfare scheme. They have a school where, for a few dollars a year, they can put in their afternoons and evenings studying the commercial branches or stenography, typewriting, cooking, sewing, household art, or music. Though not an advertised champion of the cause commonly known as "women's rights", Westinghouse always had strongly at heart the interests of the women in his employ, aiming not only to give every one of them her chance, but seeing to it that she had everything within reason done for her health and comfort. When he built his works at East Pittsburgh, almost the first thing he noticed in inspecting their outside appearance was the absence of proper sidewalks and overhead protection. "This won't do," said he. "We employ a great many women, and when it storms they will be exposed to the rain in their thin dresses, or walk in unprotected shoes from the doors to the car-tracks. They will catch cold, and if any harm comes to them it will be our fault. We must have a viaduct." So, although the buildings had already cost so much that he was under sharp criticism from his shorter-sighted stockholders, a fine steel and concrete viaduct went up without delay; and many a young woman undoubtedly owes her immunity from illness to his thoughtfulness.

Perhaps the most characteristic provision made for the girls is the lunch-room at the. Electric and Manufacturing Works, where they can take their noon meal under restful and economical conditions. It stands at the end of a spacious aisle, and contains thirty-five tables with accommodations for more than a thousand women. The tables are neatly covered with enameled oilcloth, and hot coffee, sugar, and cream are contributed by the Company, together with two maid-servants to keep the room in order, heat the coffee, wash the dishes, etc. What gives it its distinctive Westinghouse touch is the way the work of attendance is methodized so that the two maids can do it all without difficulty. The coffee is heated in fifteen-gallon urns, and carried to the tables on a truck specially designed for the purpose, provided with pneumatic tires and springs to prevent breaking or chipping the chinaware; and when the lunchers disperse the dishes go into a machine operated by a motor and controlled by one of the maids, which washes and dries them automatically.

The fact that the works of the Air Brake Company, the Union Switch and Signal Company, the Electric and Manufacturing Company, and the Machine Company, though in separate boroughs, practically adjoin one another along a line of railroad that runs through Turtle Creek Valley, not only gives them a community of interest in many matters, but facilitates official inspection, encourages the social mingling of the employees, and fosters the adoption by one company of the advanced ideas of another as soon as they have proved their worth by experiment. As a result, not infrequently a capable workman in one of the Westinghouse plants has been asked by his neighbors to accept office as burgess or councilor and has made a most creditable public record.

Naturally, where fifty thousand men and women are employed, more than half the number at some specialized form of skilled industry, the eternal labor question has not held itself aloof. Agitators have from time to time tried to stir up strife between managers and men, but with little effect. It was the consistent policy of George Westinghouse to treat with his own workmen, neither interfering in the affairs of other employers nor himself submitting to any dictation from without. His general attitude with regard to the important question of organized labor is a matter of record. Statements have been erroneously made that he opposed it. He recognized the absolute right of men to form associations for protective and beneficial purposes, holding strongly, however, to the view that there should be no interference with the rights of those who were not thus associated. This position was well reflected in the correspondence he had with Samuel Gompers in April, 1903. Mr. Gompers wrote that he had been informed that the Westinghouse interests were opposed to union labor. Mr. Westinghouse answered that all the managers of his companies were earnestly striving to better existing conditions and always ready to lend a helping hand; adding:

"They are a unit with me in wishing that our employees should not join such organizations as would render them liable to be involved in agitations or disputes which have no reference to their work or their employment with the Westinghouse Companies. All workmen are guaranteed the same rights and privileges with us, whether they are affiliated with organized labor or not."

He firmly believed that all the advantages, with practically none of the drawbacks that go with the ordinary labor unions, could be realized by a union formed of the employees of each manufacturing industry without affiliation with other similar organizations. This, in effect, is the condition existing at the Air Brake Works. All the virtues of what is called "collective bargaining" are available for the benefit of its employees, and the Company, on its part, is enabled to take broader views and adopt more liberal policies than if it were hampered by outside influences having no real knowledge of the business or conditions surrounding it.

In short, by maintaining a high standard of wages, encouraging the operatives to make this continuously possible by turning out the finest quality of products in the market, and providing for the welfare of the old and infirm workmen, Westinghouse avoided any serious labor trouble. As we have already seen, when financial clouds hung over him as head of a great company, his employees hastened to the rescue in a spirit that reflected equal credit upon them and him. No man who applied for work had ever been questioned as to his membership of a trade union, a church, or a political party, and none had been discharged except for cause, or — as happened in a few instances for a brief period — because business was too dull to permit of carrying the maximum force. Even here, however, "the Old Man's" kindness of heart occasionally played a part at odds with his selfish advantage. Such was the case when the year 1896, opening with slack prospects, found the Electric and Manufacturing Company's works so overmanned that, in the interest of prudence, four or five hundred laborers were likely to be laid off in midwinter. Westinghouse sent for one of his lieutenants and inquired into the matter. When he saw how serious the situation was, he said:

"I am going away for a while, but I can't leave till I have made some arrangement for continuing those men at work, at least till the cold weather is over. Haven't we anything in the shops that needs over hauling?"

"No, sir," answered the man, "not a thing that I know of now."

"What has become of that load of stuff we put into the loft some time ago to get it out of the way?"

"It is there still, and it's practically all scrap. There's nothing in the lot that we could possibly make use of by repairing it."

"Well, never mind, get it down and do something to it — I don't care much what, as long as these fellows are employed. If that won't answer, bring out some billets and have them shaped into squares or hexagons."

"But, Mr. Westinghouse, it would mean a tremendous waste."

"No, it wouldn't. Nothing will be wasted that keeps the wives and children of all these men from suffering this winter. Do as I tell you."

And his orders were obeyed, with the result that hundreds of workmen remained on the pay roll through the inclement season with nothing but humanity as an excuse for keeping them there.

Again, in 1899, about a dozen faithful employees of the Air Brake Company attained the age of seventy just before they had finished the full twenty years' service required to entitle them to pensions. According to its strict letter, the rule must have been enforced against them on the 9th of September, and they would have lost their pensions though too old to remain in the Company's service or to obtain work elsewhere. When, almost at the last moment, Mr. Westinghouse learned of their plight, he at once called the directors together, and, by the force of his personal influence, procured an amendment to the regulations postponing till the 1st of October the date when the exclusion rule must take effect.

A like trait manifested itself in other ways. Once he descended with such vigor upon a new mechanic who had spoiled a minor casting that the offender, who had not yet had a chance to "measure the Old Man up", was nervously unstrung. A more experienced associate consoled him by saying: "Oh, the Boss doesn't really mean much by that. The next time he starts to roast you, just tell him your wife is sick." It was a familiar proverb at the works that any tale of distress among his employees aroused the sympathy of Westinghouse at once, and changed his severity to gentleness.

He had become interested in a copper mine in Arizona, when a neighboring customs officer, smitten with a spasm of superserviceable zeal, swooped down upon the property and arrested about thirty of the unnaturalized Mexican miners on a groundless charge, threw them into a local jail in midsummer, and began a criminal prosecution against their employer. As soon as the news reached Westinghouse that the unfortunates were suffering maltreatment, he ignored all considerations of his own possible loss, and concentrated his entire attention on the fate of his men, telegraphing his representative on the ground to bail them out at any cost and see that no further harm came to them. The case was eventually dropped by the Government, but not till Westinghouse had spent a great deal of money in undoing the effect of this act of official stupidity.

With all his generosity of spirit, he could not forgive ingratitude. A poor Hungarian who had recently come to the works and could speak almost no English was suffering from an ulcerated tooth which grew steadily worse till the doctor told him he could get no relief except from a serious operation. The man was in despair. He could not afford the sacrifice of wages which would be involved in his taking time off to go to a hospital, and he feared that, with his ignorance of our language, he might not be able to find another place if he lost this one. Westinghouse, as soon as his case was made known, ordered that he be sent to a hospital and his wages paid him during his absence, and also gave him a sum of money to meet any unforeseen expense to which he might be put before his recovery.

On the strength of this incident, one of the higher paid employees, an Austrian who had grown homesick, was moved to play upon the sympathies of so kind a patron, and worked up a mock case of stomalgia, for which a sea voyage and a visit to a certain specialist in Austria were said to hold forth the only hope of a cure. Down went Westinghouse's hand into his pocket and the man was sent abroad by the next available steamer. After a pleasant sojourn at his old home he returned, and in an expansive mood boasted to some of his boon companions how he had "played it on the Old Man." The story reached Westinghouse's ears and the swindler was packed off with incredible speed. As his position in the works was one that required a peculiar training, he was unable to find other employment without a certificate of merit, but when it came to granting any kind of concession he found the soft heart of his employer turned as hard as flint.

CHAPTER XIX

A TRIO OF HOMES

IN the matter of homes George Westinghouse was more than commonly favored, having three that were permanent and two that were movable. In the permanent homes, at Pittsburgh, Pennsylvania, Lenox, Massachusetts, and Washington, D. C., his wife was the presiding genius, and her word there was law. Of the temporary homes, one was a hotel in New York City, liable to change from year to year; the other was a private railway car called the Glen Eyre, with commodious sleeping quarters, dining room, kitchen, and office. Wherever he might be, this was always held in readiness for his occupancy, with his secretary and other companions, and, attached to the most convenient train, it bore him hither and yon without interruption of any business he happened to have in hand at the time

As we have already seen, his house on the eastern outskirts of Pittsburgh was bought in 1871. It was built of brick, in the villa style of architecture, with the square tower and Mansard roof then so popular, and stood in the midst of an attractive plot of ground on a slight eminence close to the local railway station, so that he had only a few minutes' walk to reach the train which bore him daily into the city. To avoid

a more roundabout route in descending to the level
on which the tracks ran, he laid out a cross-path from
the house door to the corner of the lawn, and built
a small tunnel from that point to the station. To
this estate Mrs. Westinghouse had given the name
Solitude, because that seemed most appropriate
to the retreat where nightly her husband could separate himself from the noise and bustle of the rushing
world in which he passed his days. When they first
moved into the house they had not the means to
furnish all of it, so the drawing-room was left as it
was, and a smaller room on the opposite side of the
entrance hall was fitted for social and family purposes. Later, as their circumstances improved,
they had the whole house refurnished with some
elaborateness, besides extending it to the rear so as
to add a spacious and high-ceiled dining room.
Westinghouse's favorite place for sitting with his
friends during the winter season was a square hall a
little back from the main entrance, flanked by an
angular staircase and containing an open fireplace.
In the warm weather he enjoyed spending his evenings on the porch. He was always a happy host,
and rarely a day passed when a few of his friends —
most frequently his business associates and their
wives — did not dine with him. When some especially perplexing question was occupying his mind,
he might slip away from the party after dinner and
seek a little library upstairs where he could be quiet
and concentrate his thoughts for a while. If he and
his guests had become involved in a discussion which
could be illuminated by a diagram, he would call

them into the billiard room and spread his papers on the green baize table, over which the group would bend with their heads close together, sometimes for an hour or more.

When I was at Solitude early in 1915, the house stood just as he and his wife had left it, except that it had been stripped of most of the finer furniture, and the bric-a-brac and curios with which they had filled it as souvenirs of their repeated trips to the old world. The walls sent back echoes of every footstep, and there was a ghostly suggestion as one walked through it and came suddenly upon a huge photograph of Mr. and Mrs. Westinghouse as they appeared during their first sojourn in London. The two figures were about one quarter life-size, and the husband's face, with its heavy crown of dark hair and its drooping mustache, appeared in profile, looking down at his wife, who was seated in front of him with her full face turned to the observer. The resemblance of the George Westinghouse of the '70's to the George Westinghouse of forty years later was so strong as to be fairly haunting. Another potent reminder of him was to be found in the festoons of webbing-sheathed wires which followed the lines of the entry ceiling and mounted to the second story; for, when he had the house equipped for electric lighting, he forbade the mechanics to cut into the woodwork, insisting on having the wires left free so that he could make any changes he wished when he believed he had hit upon a new idea. Thus he tested by actual experience every suggestion in the line of lighting that came into his mind.

At one side of the house was a vegetable garden, and in front were Mrs. Westinghouse's flower beds and a winding grape trellis. At the rear was a stable, in the cellar of which, as the premises were gradually improved, were placed the lighting and heating plants, the wires and pipes being conducted to the house through a subway large enough for a man to walk in. The construction of this underground passage furnished a lively sensation for the Pittsburgh newspapers, which ventured all kinds of guesses as to its purpose. By that time Westinghouse had become so prominent a figure locally that some of the press commentators, knowing his distaste for ordinary publicity, felt sure he was taking this means of making his way back and forth without observation while engaged on some new invention.

It was at Solitude that the natural gas experiment was made, as described in an earlier chapter. It was here, also, that many distinguished guests from abroad were entertained when attracted to Pittsburgh by what they had heard of the wonderful system of administration in its mills and shops. Conspicuous among them were Prince Albert, now King of the Belgians, and Lord Kelvin, between whom and Westinghouse had sprung up a very warm friendship, having its origin in their community of tastes and interests.

The Massachusetts home was not acquired till some time in the '80's, when Mrs. Westinghouse, whose health had for some time been not of the best, was advised by her physicians to try the effect of mountain air, and with her husband passed a large part of one season in the heart of the Berkshire Hills. Both Mr. and Mrs. Westinghouse became fascinated with the country about Lenox, and, after giving it a fair trial, Mrs. Westinghouse expressed a wish that they had a country home in such a place where she could spend her summers, living most of the time in the open air and directing the improvement and care of the grounds. They looked together over a number of eligible sites, and presently fixed upon the Schenck farm, situated in the corner where the towns of Lenox, Lee, and Stockbridge come together, and comprising about one hundred acres with a well-built house already on it. This property they bought in November, 1887. The next year they bought an adjoining piece of the Clark farm, containing some forty-one acres and a number of buildings, and the year after that another tract of twelve acres from the Smith estate, bordered for a considerable stretch by a shore of Laurel Lake. With this they rested for a while, employing the interval in improving the land they had purchased and watching for a good opportunity to obtain other parcels along the lakeside. Their chance did not come for ten years, and then a series of purchases, mostly on the shore, more than doubled their holdings. Thereafter additions were made at irregular intervals, till by the end of 1911 this estate, which they had named Erskine Park in honor of Mrs. Westinghouse's family name, compassed a total of nearly six hundred acres. The Schenck house had been enlarged and made over to fit the needs of its new owners, and the family had established themselves there in October, 1890.

The combination of climate, surroundings, and occupation proved most beneficial to Mrs. Westinghouse. Always fond of flowers, she came to take an almost childlike delight in all growing things; and here were lawns to be laid out, old trees to be trimmed or thinned, saplings to be transplanted, and shrubbery to be disposed so as to produce certain landscape effects. The estate must be supplied also with driveways and paths, the slopes would need proper grading, swamp land would have to be made wholesome, and dry soil provided with means of water. All this meant a deal of unskilled labor supplementary to the initial work of trained engineers and gardening experts; the task extended over a series of years, and Mrs. Westinghouse welcomed the chance it afforded her to help many poor fellows who lost their employment by the panic of 1893, and whose families would have suffered but for some such godsend.

How much good her own share of this work did her was shown when the improvements had reached a stage which called for the enclosure of the park, and a man was summoned from Pittsburgh to take measurements for a fence. He was somewhat amused when Mrs. Westinghouse, the semi-invalid of a few years before, proposed to accompany him on his walk around the park, so as to advise with him regarding certain details; but his amusement gave way to astonishment when she not only made the circuit without any apparent discomfort, but actually walked him down, so that he had to stop and rest before his tour was complete.

One of the least attractive features of the line

Erskine Manor, the Lenox Residence

where the Schenck and Clark farms met was a marshy tract, studded in part with half-matured willows. The suggestion that she drain this and carry the water off in tiles was too purely utilitarian to appeal to her, and she decided to turn the swamp into a lake, drawing upon Laurel Lake for whatever additional water was needed, and with a bit of judicious pruning, use the willow copse as part of a picturesque background of foliage. As the artificial lake, following with its boundaries the lines of the water-charged soil, was narrow in parts, a few bridges were thrown across the straits. Two of these, at the most exposed points, were built of marble, while the others, half hidden among the willows, were of iron, infusing into the scene, with their weblike construction and their half concealment among the trees, a Japanese effect.

When it came to running the lines of the paths and roadways, Mrs. Westinghouse had a most definite conception of what she wished. The engineers arrived with their technical instruments, prepared to do everything themselves; but she went out every day and worked with them, directing instead of taking directions. She preferred a homely device of rope and pegs to the best brass and glass apparatus they could bring, and with her own hands she would hold the end of a rope while the men swung it around and marked its course with stakes till they had got every curve just to suit her. Sixty acres of the level part of the park was devoted to ornamental lawn, and a considerable area on the upland to a deer paddock. In the midst of one of the broad stretches near the lake was built a pavilion, where band con-

certs were given occasionally on fine summer afternoons. There were tennis courts close by, also.

A distinguishing mark of Erskine Park was its
system of white carriage drives. They were visible
from the public highway, and never failed to excite
comment from strangers passing the gates. Their
whiteness was due to the finely crushed marble used
for surfacing them. Soon after purchasing the land
for the estate, Mr. Westinghouse selected a site for
a deep well, and started drilling, but at a depth of
five hundred feet ran into a "cap" of marble, of the
same quality as the product of the famous Lee
quarries. With the eye of the ever practical man,
he saw at once the use to which this could be put,
and took a constant satisfaction in the sense that
there never could be any neglect of the upkeep of his
drives without his promptly discovering the blot on
the pure white surface.

A big barn stood near the house when the Schenck
place was bought, and, as it was not required for its
original purposes, a question arose as to its disposal.
One rainy day Mrs. Westinghouse went out to look
it over, and was struck with the idea of turning it
into a recreation-house. Accordingly the mows and
bins were emptied, the lower ground floor — for the
building stood on two levels — was fitted up with
pantry and kitchen appliances, dressing rooms, and
the like, and the entire upper ground floor was cleared
of permanent obstructions and equipped for a gigantic
club or living room, with books and pictures, card
tables and lounging chairs everywhere, and gymnastic
apparatus, a bowling alley and a billiard table so

placed as to be least in the way if the floor had to be cleared for dancing, a reception, or a hunt breakfast.

Against the wall were hung from time to time numberless framed photographs, many of them bearing the autographs of their subjects or of the artists who took them, and nearly every one having a story connected with it. Here were portraits of musicians and actors, men of letters and doctors in various sciences with whom the family were on terms of friendship. Mingled with these were the portraits of relatives or childhood associates, and one of an interesting girl in whom George Westinghouse believed he had discovered a genius, and whom he sent abroad for a thorough education in music. For perfection of workmanship, the amateur photographs of Albert Kapteyn, a Dutch gentleman, easily bore off the palm; their subjects were of the genre order, but most of them were outdoor views in Holland, England, Scotland, Belgium, Germany, Switzerland, and Spain.

On the tops of the bookshelves were grouped a few of the hunting trophies obtained by the present George Westinghouse while a lad. He had importuned his parents for a gun till at last his mother consented to give him one if he would agree to shoot only a single specimen of any kind of wild creature. Under this contract he brought her his birds and beasts, and she had them mounted by a taxidermist and added to the collection of family memorials.

Mrs. Westinghouse took the keenest pride in what she jocosely termed her farming. Live stock was her special hobby, and she was a regular exhibitor at the annual horse show in Lenox. Her farm horses, which never failed to receive some flattering award, carried off in one year the first, second, and third prizes. The walls of her greenhouses bristled with certificates from the Lenox Horticultural Society, of honors won by her gardener, Edward J. Norman, for his displays at the local Florist Show. Her herd of fine milch cows, varying in number from twenty to twenty-five, paid their tribute to a dairy built and equipped on the most modern plans, and run in every department by electricity. This was for several years one of the special objects of interest for visitors at the Park, partly because of the novelty of the mechanical devices employed, and partly because the barnyard was surfaced with the same crushed marble as was used on the carriage drives, giving the whole place an air of aggressive cleanliness.

"The Lenox residence," writes an old family friend, "was Mrs. Westinghouse's idea in every detail, and was the first building in the world, so far as I know, in which diffused electric lighting was attempted, the effect being to give the appearance of daylight, there being no shadows in any room. The lamps were arranged, throughout the house and on the piazzas, in a special moulding where the walls joined the ceilings. There were some fifteen hundred lamps in all, every one made especially for Mrs. Westinghouse, as were also the sockets, switches, and other appliances. When you reflect that this took place thirty years ago, you get an idea of the magnitude of the undertaking. I recall that even Mr. Westinghouse, in spite of his progressive ideas, opposed his wife in this matter, but she carried out her plan, with a result much admired and quickly copied; and as in 1888 electric lighting in private residences was in its infancy, and the few lamps were usually hung on the gas fixtures without even the concealment of the wires, some conception of the innovation is possible. This was brought home to me about fifteen years later, when one of the engineers from the Electric Works in Pittsburgh came to Erskine Park to report on the electric light plant. Just before starting back, he asked if he might go into the house and see the arrangement of the lights — a surprising request in view of the progress that had been made in interior electric lighting since this house was built. He explained that he was working in the shops when the apparatus was made, that everything was special because nothing like it had ever been made before, and no one there could understand how it was to be used; so he determined that if he ever got within a hundred miles of the place he would see the results.''

The electric energy employed on the estate generally was supplied from a power house situated in a retired nook at the north end of the estate. This was a substantial stone structure, containing a complete steam plant and dynamos for generating current. A rotary pump operated by an electric motor lifted from Laurel Lake the water needed for feeding the artificial lake, and on more than one occasion came to the rescue when the public water company at Lenox found itself crippled by some emergency. To this establishment, also, Lenox was indebted for the introduction of electric lighting into the village.

The Westinghouse home in Washington was the fine brick mansion on the west side of Dupont Circle built by James G. Blaine when he became Secretary of State in the Garfield Cabinet, but unused by him, owing to the assassination of the President and his own withdrawal for a season from public life. It was leased for several years to Levi Z. Leiter, the retired merchant from Chicago, and then passed into possession of Mrs. Westinghouse. Here the family lived for a series of winters, taking a lively interest in the social and benevolent activities of the city, particularly while the McKinleys were in the White House. It was in this house that Mrs. Westinghouse gave a demonstration of her executive ability which attracted the widest attention.

In the spring of 1899 the American Society of Mechanical Engineers was to hold a convention in Washington, and it was the desire of Mr. Westinghouse, as one of the recognized pillars of the organization, to entertain his fellow members in some way. He accordingly issued invitations for a large reception, which was to give them an opportunity to meet the chief dignitaries of the Government and the resident diplomatic corps; but these were hardly out before he received a sudden summons abroad and was obliged to take passage on the next steamer. The situation was critical, for the signs all forecast an enormous attendance, and not a move had been made toward arranging a program or preparing the house. Mrs. Westinghouse stepped at once into the breach. Perceiving that, capacious as her main floor was, it could not accommodate such an assemblage with comfort, she had a ballroom thrown out to cover the entire garden in the rear, practically doubling her space. It was built of wood, but elaborately decorated inside, with an expansive effect produced by a series of arches; and so cleverly was its point of juncture with the main house concealed, that no one unfamiliar with the premises suspected that it was merely a temporary structure.

Every detail of her plan was executed under her personal supervision, and at the head of the receiving line she welcomed more than three thousand guests who would not have assumed from her appearance or manner that such momentous undertakings were not with her an everyday experience. At her side stood Rear Admiral Melville, president of the society. Until that evening he had always cherished a rather unflattering impression of women as administrators, especially in emergencies calling for rapid thought and action on a broad scale; but he confessed to his friends after this reception, the largest of the season in a city of large functions, that he was a convert to the opposite view.

Westinghouse was eminently a domestic man. He had no taste for club life, but aimed to make his home his place of refreshment. Mrs. Westinghouse did all she could to encourage this idea. Her household management was on so elastic a plan that when her husband would suddenly telephone her, as he often did, that he was going to bring two, six, or even ten friends home to dinner, nothing went awry.

The conversation at their table never took a turn toward ill-natured or meddling gossip. It was light or grave according to who might be present; but when he had his choice, Westinghouse liked to talk about the latest news from the technical world, or what would happen next in commerce or politics. Mrs. Westinghouse recognized that her first usefulness as a partner of her husband lay in making his path as smooth as possible and enabling him to devote his best faculties to his work, secure from any petty worries that could be avoided. And she carried the same spirit into larger matters also, for, when his business troubles reached their crisis in 1907, she came forward at once with all the securities he had made over to her at various times as gifts, and insisted upon throwing them into the general pool to help relieve his embarrassment.

In return, his devotion to her throughout their married life was chivalry itself. She could not express a wish that he did not lay himself out to gratify, whether it seemed to him wise or whimsical. When they were separated he never allowed a night to pass without exchanging a few words with her by telephone or telegraph, usually about the happenings of the day. It made no difference whether they were on the same side of the ocean or not. He cabled her from London early one evening that Lord and Lady Kelvin and several other guests were coming to dine with him, and received her answer, extending her greetings to the company, before they sat down to table. His habit in this regard was much facilitated by the installation of private wires in every house they occupied, connecting it with his distant business offices. When he was at home, these enabled him to communicate promptly and confidentially with his subordinates; when he was away, they afforded a means of reaching his wife without the delays incident to ordinary messages. At Erskine Park the long-distance telephone was brought even into the dressing room to which the golf players resorted after a game.

Of buoyant temperament himself, Westinghouse had no use for pessimists, but wished about him only cheerful persons, with happy, hopeful faces and ways. He was fond of young people, and was rarely without one or more in his home. He liked especially to have his nieces about, and used to call them, because they were so merry, his "patent gigglers." All the good stories he heard during his absences he saved for the amusement of his wife, and often sent friends to her to hear them retold in her version.

CHAPTER XX

Insignia of Character

Soon after the receivers were appointed in 1907, George Westinghouse one morning with a friend was on a train passing the Air Brake Works at Wilmerding, and the shops of the Electric and Manufacturing and Machine Companies at East Pittsburgh. He had been reading some newspaper comments on his misfortunes, in which admiration for his genius and character was tempered with charitable reflections on his lack of business judgment; and there was a strong flavor of sarcasm in his voice and manner as he remarked:

"They say I'm no financier." Then, after a moment's pause, and with a sweeping gesture which took in the whole industrial panorama: "So I suppose all those great works built themselves!"

His newspaper critics had touched on the quick the most sensitive spot in his make-up, for, if he cherished one pet vanity, it was his self-confidence in directing his business on its fiscal as well as its mechanical side. His resourcefulness as an inventor was due to the wonderful scope of his imagination, but that faculty often stood him in bad stead in financial affairs, for few of the men on whom he must depend for pecuniary support were able to forecast the future in his grand way, and in hours of stress when he most needed their aid they were sometimes least prepared to extend it. "Having solved to his own satisfaction the real inherent difficulties in any problem," says Calvert Townley, "his mind leaped forward over the intervening barriers to ultimate success, seeing, as if already accomplished, results which would require not only vigorous effort but considerable time. An invention that showed great promise in laboratory or shop was at once, in his mind, being successfully marketed throughout the world in quantities to which its worth would ultimately entitle it. He resented the thought of the time that must intervene to create public demand and distribute the product. What he knew to be right, he expected others to admit sooner than they did."

No manufacturing plant of his was ever built big enough to suit him; he never inspected an installation in one of his shops without beginning to calculate how soon it would be outgrown. It was a universal custom, when he entered business, to count "prospective earnings" as a legitimate part of the basis of capitalization in launching a corporate enterprise, and he simply followed the habit of his contemporaries. Moreover, he insisted on living up to this idea even when things were going against him; no matter how hard the times, dividends must be maintained when earned, for the shareholders expected them; if this involved a perilous strain on the present resources of the concern — well, it would all be made up later, so why borrow trouble? And it is but fair to admit that, as a rule, his expectations were eventually justified as to the main outcome, however injudicious it may have been at the time to trade so heavily on the future. Having fixed his purpose to achieve a certain result, he counted no outlay as extravagant if it would speed his progress to that goal. He once said to Mr. Townley: "I shall spend one hundred thousand dollars this year in developing my gas-producer."

Few persons not intimately associated with him suspected the amounts he threw without compunction into investigations and experiments which promised nothing directly in themselves, but would probably point the way for an advance in some untried direction. When his brother protested against his paying what seemed an exorbitant price for a device that he believed would help him in his work, he answered good-humoredly: "I appreciate your interest, Herman, but, all the same, I am going to do it!"

He was equally indifferent to the æsthetic appeal where it came into conflict with the practical. Frank S. Smith, a former member of his staff, says that in 1892 "there was under development in the Electric Company's Works a special grinding apparatus for use in connection with the manufacture of the 'stopper' lamp. During Mr. Westinghouse's absence, the head of one of the departments, an excellent designer, had constructed a machine which did the work fairly well and followed a very graceful design. Mr. Westinghouse, on his return, dissected the whole machine and reconstructed it on a much more effective but less artistic plan. On my assuming to remark that although the new apparatus worked very well, it did not look nearly so well as the original, he answered: "Smith, what works well looks well."

His standards were free from any taint of mere personal profit. He cared for money only because it would give him power to do big things. "Had he coveted riches for their own sake," says Mr. Stillwell, "he could have passed his life making steel rails, cutting them off in thirty-foot lengths, and selling them for cash; but this would have led nowhere." His interest in invention was practical rather than scientific. The announcement of a new discovery in mechanics or the solution of some tedious technical riddle went for little with him unless he could see how it was going to shorten a time or a distance, double a producing capacity, or promote the public safety; then he was enthusiastic.

Perhaps owing to his difficulty in gaining a hearing for his own first great invention, he always showed much consideration for budding inventors. As a result, the various Westinghouse companies have become the repository of many thousand purchased patents; and for all that gave any promise, it is safe to say, generous returns were made. The story is told in Pittsburgh of the inventor of a rat-trap who was seeking for somebody to put it upon the market for him. A prominent citizen to whom he applied admitted that it was ingenious — too ingenious, indeed, for none but an uncommonly intelligent rat could possibly find the way into it. "He looked disappointed," said this gentleman, "but brightened when I added that his device contained one little feature which I thought might be worth his showing to George Westinghouse. Somewhat dubiously he went away. When we next met I inquired whether he had followed my advice. 'Oh, yes,' he answered; 'Mr. Westinghouse didn't care anything about the trap, but he was interested in the very feature you mentioned, because it might be of use in an invention he was developing. He bought my trap, patent rights and all. I would gladly have sold it to him for a hundred dollars. He offered me three thousand and I accepted it on the spot.'"

In his business relations Westinghouse was conspicuous for frankness and old-fashioned honesty. His unwillingness to advise the electrification of the Manhattan Elevated Railway in New York before he was convinced that the time was ripe for it was paralleled by the campaign he waged for years against combustible cars and excessive speed on electric roads either above or below ground, arguing that electricity might prove a more perilous agent than steam unless the precautions he advised were observed. Though a manufacturer of electrical apparatus and a contractor for its installation, he was ready to forego tempting pecuniary profits for the sake of dealing squarely with his customers and the public.

It was the same way with the quality of his products. He would not consent to have anything go out of the Westinghouse works until it was as perfect as his men could make it. A prominent mining engineer, speaking of this trait, remarked that he never bought any but Westinghouse machinery, because it always did more than was claimed for it — a fifty horse-power machine invariably being good for seventy horse power, and other things in like proportion. In order to fortify himself in this practice, Westinghouse was regardless of time or trouble in bringing a piece of work to the desired degree of excellence. It took four years of expensive experiment to produce the four thousand horse-power locomotive for hauling trains through the Pennsylvania tunnel under the Hudson. "If George Westinghouse said it would go, it would," declared a railroad president recently, discussing one of the latest mechanical ventures of the Machine Company.

A purchaser of a lot of incandescent lamps came back to complain that they would not do the work for which he had bought them. He found his way to Westinghouse himself, who heard all he had to say, asked him several questions, and suggested a plan for setting the matter right. As soon as the visitor had gone, Westinghouse sent for the employee who had taken the order.

"That man says he told you, when he bought those lamps, what use he was going to make of them. Is it true?" he demanded.

"Yes, sir," was the hesitating answer.

"And didn't you know they were unsuitable for his purpose?"

"Why — I suppose I thought — but the order was large, and — "

"That's not the way to build up a business,"

Westinghouse broke in sternly, and cut off further parley by dismissing the offender from his employ.

On the other hand, he was very gentle in dealing with honest mistakes. "We do not discharge our men for little things," he explained to a friend who had shown surprise at his moderation. "If we were hanged for everything we did wrong, there would be few of us left."

His odd mixture of concentration and diffusion, irregularity and method, used to baffle the comprehension of observers who knew him only superficially. They could not reconcile his lack of a fixed routine of life with the precision of movement that reigned in his shops. In the Air Brake Works, where the raw material is carried from stage to stage on a sort of continuous railway, and the castings are borne away in like manner to the assembling departments, automatism in manufacture is brought to a point which is a standing marvel to visitors from the old world, accustomed to seeing human labor still preeminent. In the Electric and Manufacturing Works the cashier's office is so systematized that seventeen thousand mechanics can be paid their wages in fifteen minutes, not with cheques but in money; and the clerical force of three thousand persons is paid by cheque with corresponding expedition.

Westinghouse himself, according to Frank H. Taylor, had a faculty of mental distribution which enabled him to converse, write a note or cast up an account and dictate to a stenographer, all at the same time. This did not interfere with his ability to catch mental photographs of any happenings that interested him, and to store negatives in so orderly a fashion in his memory as to be able later to bring out the right one whenever needed. Mr. Stillwell says that, having been interrupted midway in a conversation with some one and chancing to meet the same person six months afterward, he could resume their talk just about where it had dropped. The momentary riveting of his thought on whatever he was doing was shown in a hundred little ways. Mrs. Raymond Mallary says, for instance, that he always preferred to mix his own salad dressing at dinner, and that while he was thus engaged he would only look up with a nod to any one who addressed him, postponing a more elaborate response till the dressing was finished to his satisfaction. The Reverend Doctor Fisher of Pittsburgh describes his unconscious trick, when an important thought suddenly occurred to him at table, of rubbing his chin in an absent manner, stretching himself back, and sometimes penciling a little sketch on the damask cloth.

In spite of his being so indefatigable a worker, he was content with a moderate amount of sleep in a night. During the day, even when he was apparently resting, his mind was awake. Doubtless the expenditure of so much energy with scant replenishment would have broken down almost any man of the ordinary physique and conventional habits, but Doctor Fisher, after watching its effects upon him from young manhood, ascribes his immunity to the fact that he was continually shifting his line of work. Whatever came next his hand would absorb his immediate attention : yesterday it may have been a novelty in rotary engines, today a refractory electric-lighting apparatus; tomorrow it might be something which he believed would improve his air brake. Thus no subject with which his brain busied itself was allowed to go stale. Now and then, after several hours of uncommonly hard work, he would enter the office of one of his assistants and throw himself down upon a lounge, and every one knew his habits too well to disturb him with conversation or attention of any sort till he was ready to rise and leave or to volunteer a remark.

When traveling, he would not kill time, like most of his fellow passengers, by reading, but would seat himself beside some one — it mattered not whether an acquaintance or a stranger — and in a few minutes would be shooting questions at him like bullets from a rapid-fire gun. He did not smoke, and drank no stimulant except a little wine with his dinner. Of amusements, his preference was for those which involved calculation and bodily exercise, like golf and bowling. He liked walking if he had a definite objective or congenial companionship, but cared nothing for it simply as an expedient for stretching his muscles. Fishing he enjoyed as a means of employing his hands while turning a question over in his mind. At Erskine Park, toward the close of a busy day, he would sometimes collect his tackle and start for the pond, calling out to Mrs. Westinghouse: "I'm off to get you a few fish for dinner!" Whether he caught enough for the whole table or only one or two, it was she who must be served before anybody else. Reading, aside from the daily news and an occasional magazine article on a practical topic which had stirred his curiosity, was a rare indulgence until pretty late in life, when, apparently to his own surprise, he discovered a fancy for stories which hinged upon the unravelment of a mystery. During his early and middle life he was fond of the theater, and found particular pleasure in humorous plays that contained some special feature of excellence; but in his later years, his attendance became very infrequent.

Appreciative as he was of fun, uncleanness repelled him. "At a dinner of his agents and engineers in Pittsburgh at which he was not present," says Mr. Stillwell, "some one told an off-color story, and a member of the party who had had more wine than was good for him kept calling for another still less decorous. Macfarland, who was presiding, stood the nuisance for a while, and then announced to the company that no more stories of that character should be told while he was in the chair, as Mr. Westinghouse did not approve of such things. There was loud applause; every one had such respect for 'the Old Man' that Macfarland carried his point without even a show of active opposition."

Although he never took part in politics beyond allowing his name to be used once on the Republican ticket as a Presidential Elector, his interest in public affairs was strong. As he had repeatedly proved himself a good party man, many of his friends marveled at his outspoken admiration for Grover Cleveland.

"Oh," he explained, when one of them questioned

him about it, "Mr. Cleveland is an exception to all rules. He's a good enough citizen to be a Republican!"

William McKinley had a high regard for Westinghouse's expert judgment and fairness of mind. Early in 1890, while chairman of the Ways and Means Committee of the House of Representatives, he sent Westinghouse a request for an interview on a certain day. As Westinghouse was going to Chicago on that day, he invited McKinley to join him at Pittsburgh, and accompany him on the Glen Eyre, so that they could have their interview on their way westward. Thomas B. Kerr, who was of the party, says that McKinley wished to discuss the broad subject of appliances for the protection of railway trainmen, as this was a matter with which Congress would soon have to deal. "After a few minutes' general talk," adds Mr. Kerr, "Mr. Westinghouse began, and for an hour held us spellbound with a wonderfully comprehensive and convincing exposition of the dangers attendant on railway service, their cause, their remedies, and the importance of remedying them, from the point of view not only of human safety, but of economy and efficiency of railroad operation, citing statistics and facts which were startling, and expressing views and making recommendations that showed his wide knowledge and the maturity of his conclusions. Mr. McKinley left us at Canton, Ohio, saying that in many respects the subject had assumed a new, definite, and practical aspect in his mind; and, watching with interest the subsequent course of legislation, I was not surprised to see many of Mr. Westinghouse's suggestions written into the law."

The strong friendship which developed later between the inventor and the statesman lends particular interest to a prophecy made by Westinghouse in 1894, two years before McKinley made his historic campaign against Bryan. "So powerful," said he, "will be the silver sentiment in 1896 that the Populists may carry enough States to throw the election into the House. There is danger then that the Democrats and Populists will combine and give the Presidency to some Western Democrat who is committed to free silver coinage; further, a silver Congress may be elected in 1896. As soon as the people saw that fifty cents' worth of silver could be made into a dollar just as good for ordinary purposes as a gold dollar, they would assume as a logical sequence that the same thing could be done with a bit of paper. Fiat inflation would follow free silver as surely as day follows night; and folly would follow folly till all confidence would be lost and the day of reckoning would have to come. I do not favor free silver, but it would be the smallest of the evils to be feared."

To an intimation that he did not seem very enthusiastic over popular government, he answered: "I do entertain a very high opinion of popular government. We must maintain it, too; but you may search the annals of history and you will find that the policy of success and the conduct of all great enterprises are shaped by the few. Ambition, the desire for gain, the spirit of enterprise, induce rich men to engage in undertakings which benefit the world, but which the people would never undertake in a body."

Love of country was with him a positive religion. In the center of the main lawn at Erskine Park stood, during his later years, the highest flagstaff anywhere thereabout, surmounted by two metallic circles holding electric lamps which were a beacon at night visible from every point on the surrounding roads. The pole was raised to take part in a notable celebration of Independence Day in 1898. The war with Spain had reached a crucial stage, the air was vibrant with national ardor, and it occurred to Westinghouse that this would be a good time to invite the people of the countryside, including all the school children, to come together and glorify their heritage as American citizens. So he procured the largest and finest flag he could find, ordered a carload of refreshments, sent out his invitations, and awaited with glowing anticipations the arrival of the Fourth of July, when the flag was to be raised for the first time.

But on the afternoon of the third a rumor gained circulation that an important battle had been fought off the south coast of Cuba. No particulars could be ascertained, even as to the general results, and for a while the joyful prospects for the morrow were balanced by forebodings. Westinghouse became more and more restless as the afternoon wore away, and, after drawing upon every source of information, he bethought him of the chief clerk of a hotel in Washington where he had often stayed, and which was famous as a headquarters for officers of the

Government and newspaper correspondents. To this man he telegraphed late in the evening, begging for any trustworthy information whatever about the reported battle. After midnight came the answer. The clerk, having contrived to get hold of an important naval functionary, had received a "tip" that, though most of the details were still lacking, the American fleet had won a great victory off Santiago.

Westinghouse could wait no longer. Seizing his flag, he ran out and fastened it to the halyards hanging from the pole, and hauled it up with his own hands, so that the dawn found it afloat and testifying to his enterprise as well as his patriotism.

Among the idiosyncrasies of Westinghouse, none was more marked for many years than his hatred of personal publicity. He was glad to have his industries exploited to the fullest extent, for in that direction lay commercial success; but so sedulously did he keep himself in the background that, long after he had become a celebrity in the outside world, he was practically unknown to the mass of his fellow citizens of Pittsburgh. This was because almost their only chance to see him was when he walked from the railway station to his office or from his office back to the station. He refused to let his portrait appear in the newspapers if there were any way of keeping it out. "When I want newspaper advertising," he would say, "I will order it and pay cash." Or again: "If my face becomes too familiar to the public, every bore or crazy schemer I meet in the street will insist on buttonholing me."

These facts will explain how it happened that the best photograph ever made of him was a snapshot stolen when he was unaware of what was going on. It caught his fine profile as he bent over a drawing board in the attitude of absorption so characteristic of him, and derives a special charm from his manifest unconsciousness. This satisfactory result was brought about through the connivance of two members of his staff, one of whom concealed himself with a camera in a closet opening off the room of his confederate, whither it was known that "the Old Man" was coming that morning to study some drawings. The light from an adjoining window fell just where it was wanted, and the photographer, keeping the closet door a trifle ajar, watched till his chief was thoroughly engrossed, and then pressed the button. At first Westinghouse was inclined to be indignant when he learned what a trick had been played upon him, but, as usual, his irritation did not last long.

Akin to his dislike of having his portrait published was his aversion to letting his name be used in the title of any enterprise not strictly in the line of his business. When, in 1888–1889 he removed his Air Brake Works from Pittsburgh to their present site, Wilmerding was open farm country, with no human habitations except two log houses visible in the neighborhood. Forecasting its possibilities as a manufacturing region, he purchased about five hundred acres of land, though obliged to include farms stretching from the bottoms which he could utilize back over the hillsides which he could not, for the owners were unwilling to sell him the desirable tracts unless he could buy the undesirable as well. On his establishment of the nucleus of his industrial settlement, it seemed to some of his friends most appropriate to christen it "Westinghouse", but he would not consent. Ten years later came a proposal to consolidate the boroughs of East Pittsburgh, Turtle Creek, and Wilmerding, and call the combination "Westinghouse" or "Westinghouse City", in recognition of the great changes for good which had been wrought in the whole region since he had begun to take an interest in it; but the citizens who consulted him found him still objecting. Whatever his real motive, he playfully attributed his opposition to a dread of having his name brought into all sorts of unsavory associations.

"Think how I should feel," he answered one man who was particularly persistent, "if I were to pick up my paper some morning and read an account of the arrest of John Smith of Westinghouse for burglary, or the commitment of William Jones of Westinghouse for habitual drunkenness! No, I can't permit it."

And again, when the apprentices in one of his shops organized a baseball nine and wished to call it the Westinghouse Club, he would not let them. "If you need money, boys," said he, "come to me, and I'll be glad to help you out; but you mustn't use my name."

CHAPTER XXI

"Last Scene of All"

THE Westinghouse family was remotely of Saxon stock, the original name being Westinghausen; but one branch migrated to England, and from this sprang the American line. As far back as there is any record, the men have been of fine physique. George, with his exceptionally large head, his broad shoulders, and his stalwart frame more than six feet in height, was only typical of his ancestry, to whom he never failed to give full credit when any one remarked upon his splendid vitality. Indeed, his general sense of soundness, and his belief that his temperate habits would ward off the disorders which beset most men late in life, betrayed him into occasional imprudences that caused his wife much anxiety, and not without reason.

With all his modesty of demeanor, he was a very proud man. Told once that some one had accused him of never knowing when he was beaten, he answered instantly · "Oh, yes, I should have known if I ever had been beaten, but I never have been!" The blow dealt him in 1910 by men on whose lifelong support he had confidently counted made no outward mark upon him; he faced the world after it with the same intrepid look in his eyes and the same assurance of manner that it knew so well of old; but he had suffered a wound of the spirit from which he never recovered. His reluctance to admit this, even to himself, caused him to conceal various minor ills which might have yielded to medical treatment if taken promptly in hand, but which, neglected, gradually crippled his resistant force when more threatening illness came. He would dismiss every inquiry with a casual, "Oh, it's only a cold; we all have colds sometimes," or, "I dare say I have eaten something that doesn't agree with me; it's not worth another thought." Now and then a friend would remonstrate with him so seriously as to draw out some reply like: "I can't afford to be sick — you know that; there's too much depending on me."

The first intimation he permitted to escape him that he realized his gradual weakening came one morning early in 1911 when he was ascending the approach to the entrance of the Air Brake Works at Wilmerding. Pausing a moment, he said: "I must be getting old; it tires me to walk up these steps." During a visit to Lenox the same year, he was attacked in the night with a fit of coughing which lasted two hours; not till long afterward, however, did he confess to any one that he had experienced, in the midst of the paroxysm, a sensation as if his heart had been torn loose. In the summer of 1913, while his family were in the country, he began coughing again at the dinner table, so violently that the servants were frightened, and one of them hastened to summon Doctor William A. Stewart, his Pittsburgh physician. Before the doctor arrived the spasm had so far subsided that the patient was ready to turn the whole matter aside with a witticism. But Stewart's trained eye took in more than appeared on the surface, and in response to repeated requests for permission to make a thorough physical examination, Westinghouse finally yielded a very grudging consent. It was the first time he had undergone anything of the sort since, as a youth, he enlisted in the army, and it brought to light the fact that he had a dilated heart and other organic weaknesses which meant that his life-lease was running out. In view of these discoveries he consented to drop his current work for a month and try to amuse himself at Erskine Park. Meanwhile a business associate who had long been familiar with his affairs and felt on terms that would warrant such a liberty, urged him to make a will, but for some time he could not be induced to consider the idea with any patience. It required another warning to bring him to the point.

Few of his immediate family were left to provide for. His father had died in 1890, the same strong-willed, conservative, characterful man to the last. In spite of their early disagreements as to the value of the air brake invention, and certain old-fashioned strictures of the father on what he regarded as the extravagances of the son, they had always remained the warmest of friends. The mother, who after middle life had become a semi-invalid, had in her widowhood been a member of her son's household till her death in 1895. The sisters were all gone. Of the brothers, only the youngest remained, Jay and John having died within a few months of their father.

Notwithstanding the business ordeal through which he had passed but a few years before, Westinghouse still retained a considerable estate, the bulk of which his will divided between his wife, his son, and his brother Henry Herman in various proportions. He remembered generously, also, some of his faithful subordinates who had stood in close relations with him, and the older family servants, and canceled all debts owing him by other persons. Henry Herman Westinghouse, Charles A. Terry, his old friend and counsel, and Walter D. Uptegraff, who had for many years acted as his secretary and financial adviser, he made his executors, without bonds, and with practically unlimited discretion in the handling of the property. He left no outside benefactions, a fact sufficiently explained by his well-understood philosophy of giving. When Thomas B. Kerr once asked his aid for a mission church which was doing good work among the iron-mill hands in the outskirts of Pittsburgh, he contributed the sum needed, but only on condition that his identity should not be divulged. "Then," Mr. Kerr related, "he turned to me and said: 'I have never permitted my name to be associated with any such subscription list. I am convinced from observation and experience that the greater part of the money which is given for benevolence is a detriment rather than a help, for it tends to pauperize the recipient by destroying his honest pride of independence, and adds to the burden of society by the development of a class of people who are willing to accept charity rather than to exercise their own ability. I think, as a rule, a dollar given to a man does him ten dollars' worth of harm, while a dollar honestly earned by his own efforts does him ten dollars' worth of good; so my ambition is to give as many persons as possible an opportunity to earn money by their own efforts, and this has been the reason why I have tried to build up corporations which are large employers of labor, and to pay living wages, larger even than other manufacturers pay, or than the open labor market necessitates.'

"It is a matter of history, of course, how Mr. Westinghouse carried out this idea. Thereafter his apparent ambition to build up large concerns had a different aspect in my eyes, as I understood the ethical impulse underlying it. While he disclaimed belief in the efficacy of benevolent giving, and shrank from acknowledgment of his kindness, those of us who were closely connected with him knew of many instances where he was supporting whole families and doing other deeds of helpfulness in an unostentatious way. Mrs. Westinghouse was very sympathetic and loved to relieve distress, and Mr. Westinghouse made her a regular allowance for the gratification of her desires in this respect. The amount was stated to me, and it was large."

The play spell at Lenox, though extended to three times its proposed length, did not accomplish what some of the more optimistic friends of the family, regardless of the doctor's dictum, had been hoping it would. When Westinghouse returned to his office, his lieutenants were shocked at the change for the worse that had come over his appearance. Most of the color had left his face; his manner, once so brisk, had become languid; and he would doze over his work or during any brief lapse in a conversation. He walked little, and then with the slow step of a tired man. To the doctor, who at his instance had made a second physical examination, he related an incident of his country sojourn, of which a rumor had reached Pittsburgh, but the full significance of which had not been appreciated. It appeared that he had gone one morning to the pond for an hour's fishing, and sought his rowboat at the usual mooring, unaware that it had been taken away for repairs and another left in its place. The substitute was keelless, and, as he stepped into it, turned over, throwing him into the pond. Fortunately he was where the water was only chin-deep, and the mooring was close to a bridge, upon which he laid hold as an aid in clambering out; but the bank was steep just there, his weight was considerably more than two hundred pounds, and the strain which this exertion put upon his heart was excessive.

Two of his nieces were playing tennis a short distance away, and in his desire to escape their notice he took a roundabout route to the house in his wet clothes. That night he went to bed with a severe cold that lingered for weeks, and caused fits of coughing which harassed him so that he dreaded to go to sleep, lest he should be seized with a paroxysm and strangle before he could summon assistance. To add to his distress, he felt that it was important to keep his wife in ignorance of his condition, her own being such that any violent shock was liable to cause her death.

Once more Doctor Stewart protested against his continuing his work, but he insisted that he must settle the affairs of the Security Investment Company and sever his direct connection with it. As he explained that this might make all the difference between adequate and inadequate provision for his creditors and family after he was gone, the doctor consented. That business finished, Westinghouse agreed to leave Pittsburgh for a while if the doctor would accompany him, and in November, 1913, they went together to Erskine Park. Stewart's companionship on the journey and during their stay in Lenox seemed to revive a good deal of the old sprightliness in Westinghouse, who, except when his illness took on an acute phase, told stories and jested like his former self. The doctor slept in a chamber adjoining his, and frequently looked in upon him during the night, almost always finding him quiet but wide awake; the sleeplessness which had grown out of his apprehensions of some months before seemed now to have become a settled habit.

The moods of the patient increased to fitfulness as his strength slipped away. He lost his appetite for the food prescribed for him, and, in his long despondent periods, would beg the doctor to let him die unless he could be allowed to resume work. At other times he would take a cheerful view of what he now realized was the inevitable end of his trial, even getting back a little of his whimsical humor.

One nourishing compound which it was hard work at the outset to lure him into swallowing he presently came to relish. Its chief ingredient was a raw egg, and when he was ready for a glass of it he would give the signal by asking: "Doctor, isn't it time for me to cackle?"

After Christmas, he hoped to be able to go to his Washington home, which he had extensively repaired. With this plan in view the first stage of the journey was made to New York, but there the party took a suite in the Hotel Langham for the rest of the winter, as it seemed unwise to proceed further for the present.

About the beginning of March matters seemed to be temporarily at a standstill, but soon afterward he was taken with a sinking turn and fell into a mental stupor. This remained his condition until the twelfth, when, in the midst of a crisp, bright, sunny morning, the end came, and so peacefully that the friends gathered about him were scarcely conscious of his passing. He was in a wheeled reclining chair, as if he were merely taking a rest between activities. It was the way he would have preferred to die had he been permitted to arrange the conditions himself, surrounded with none of the accessories we associate with death.

Two days later, in the presence of an assemblage which filled the Fifth Avenue Presbyterian Church, the funeral services were held, under the conduct of the pastor, the Reverend Doctor J. H. Jowett, assisted by the Reverend Doctor Samuel J. Fisher of Pittsburgh. At Woodlawn Cemetery, where the burial was private, Doctor Fisher conducted the services. For these few hours all work was suspended in the Westinghouse shops and offices in this country and in Europe, as a tribute of respect to the fallen chief. Besides large delegations from the leading scientific and engineering societies of America, more than fifty members of the Westinghouse Air Brake Veterans' Association were present; some of these men had worked for the Air Brake Company for forty years, and all had been members of its force in the first shop it occupied in Pittsburgh. The active pallbearers were eight old employees: Christopher Horrocks, Edward B. Cushing, Samuel D. Sleeth, William J. Hague, Samuel McClain, Thomas Campbell, J. Hunter Sleeth, and J. B. Brooks. The honorary pallbearers were men of distinction in business and public life, including Charles Francis Adams, Senator George T. Oliver, Rear-Admiral Robert E. Peary, Samuel Rea, and Frederick D. Underwood, besides a number of old friends and managers of the various Westinghouse companies.

In June Mrs. Westinghouse followed her husband, as the result of a third stroke of paralysis, the first of which had occurred in 1912. She left no will, her estate passing to her son and sole heir, George Westinghouse, who had married in 1909 Violet, daughter of Sir Thomas Brocklebank of Irton Hall, Cumberland, England, and had two children, George Thomas and Aubrey Harold Westinghouse. On December 15, 1915, the remains of the eminent inventor and his wife were removed to the Arlington National Cemetery, opposite Washington, D. C., where a simple but dignified marble monument marks their grave, bearing this inscription :

1846 — GEORGE WESTINGHOUSE — 1914

ACTING THIRD ASSISTANT ENGINEER, U. S. NAVY, 1864–1865

HIS WIFE

1842 — MARGUERITE ERSKINE WALKER — 1914

Here we take leave of one who was probably the most remarkable industrial leader and prophet this country has ever produced. Everything to which he addressed his energies brought forth some result for the advancement of civilization; even those experiments which ended in apparent failure contributed in their way, either as warning signals to later comers or as incentives to fresh efforts which did succeed. It was characteristic of the man that after the hand of death had been laid upon him, and he who had once been a model of virile strength could no longer move about at will, he was constantly busy with pad and pencil. The very shortcomings of the wheel-chair in which he was doomed to pass so many weary days kept his mind active, because he read in them a further opportunity to be useful; and the special task he set himself was to design a model invalid chair in which the patient could be wheeled or rocked, raised or lowered, or shifted into any position which would make him more comfortable — all by an electric mechanism under his own control.

Doctor Fisher in his funeral sermon quoted these lines:

> "I know the night is near at hand;
> The mist lies low on sea and bay;
> The autumn leaves go drifting by·
> But I have had the day."

George Westinghouse had had the day. He had filled every hour of it with achievement, and the sun when it set saw him still at work.

INDEX

ACCIDENTS, evidence of, against electricity, 96
Acheson, U. S. circuit judge, 167
Adams, Charles Francis, 298
Adams, Edward D., 173
Air, first suggestion of use of compressed, for brake, 55
Atkins, Edwin F., 217
Automatic brake, 87, 92
Automobile, compressed-air springs in, 221

BAGGALEY, RALPH, 59, 62, 73, 246
Baring Brothers' failure, 157
Belfield, Reginald, 135
Belmont, August, 202
Blaine, James G., 270
Brake, improving the speed of the, 49; the old-fashioned hand, 47
British experiments, 84; triumph of American over, 191
Brocklebank, Sir Thomas, 298
Brooks, J. B., 298
Brown, Harold P., 145, 153
Burlington, Iowa, brake testing at, 92–98; perfection of brake at, 95–98

CALDWELL, JOHN, 73, 126
Campbell, Thomas, 298
Canal, electric motive power for Erie, 176
Card, W. W., 66
Cassatt, Andrew J., 65, 202
Cataract Commission Company, 173
Central Bridge, N. Y., 1
Clark's chain brakes, 86
Cleveland, Grover, 200, 283
Cockran, William Bourke, 154
Colburn, Zerah, 77
Columbian Exposition of 1893, 162; size of contract for lighting, 169

Cornell, ex-Governor Alonzo B., 147
Cravath, Paul D., 201
Current, alternating vs. continuous electric, 132
Curtis, Leonard E., 166
Curtis, Newton M., 154
Cushing, Edward B., 298

DALZELL, JOHN, 123
Dewing, Arthur S., 217
Dooley, C. R., 251
Dredge, J., 77; a skeptical British editor, 82

EDISON, THOMAS A., 148, 150, 151, 165
Edison Medal, awarded Westinghouse, 197
Electric current, alternating, making newspaper sensation, 144; controversy over, 151; alternating triumphant among scientists in New York, 148
Electric death penalty, 152
Electric wires underground, advocated, 147
Engines, steam turbine, 183
Equitable Life Assurance Society, 198
Evershed, Thomas, 172
Experiments in switching and signaling, 102

FERRARI, ELECTRICIAN, 141
Fish, Frederick P., 166
Fisher, Rev. Dr. Samuel J., 281, 297
Flower, Gov. Roswell P., 176
Forbes, George, 174
Frick, Henry C., 202

GAS, NATURAL, 106; explosion of, at Solitude, 109; great force of, 112; in Pittsburgh industries, 114; perils of using, 115; improvements in piping, 116; Pittsburgh's problem of, 119; accident at Solitude, 121; corporation for rule of, 125; for industrial purposes, 128
Gaulard, Lucien, 135
Gerry, Elbridge T., 152
Gibbs, John Dixon, 135
Gillespie, T. A., 126, 161
Gompers, Samuel, 253
Grant, Hugh J., 150

HAGUE, WILLIAM J., 298
Herr, H. T., 187, 208
Hewitt, Abram S., 145
Hickok, President Laurens Perseus, 39
Higgins, Governor, 198
Hill, Gov. David B., 152
Hill, James J., 202
Horrocks, Christopher, 246, 298
Hughes, Charles E., 198
Humbert I, King of Italy, 193
Hyde, Henry B., 198

INSURANCE, LIFE, scandal, 198
International Niagara Commission, 173
International Railway Congress, 194

JEWETT, THOMAS L., 67
Jowett, Rev. Dr. J. H., 297

KAPTEYN, ALBERT, 267
Kelvin, Lord, 174
Kemmler, William, the Murderer, 153
Kerr, Thomas B., 166, 284, 293
Knickerbocker Trust Co., New York, failure of, 208

LAMP, the Sawyer-Man, 162, 167; the Stopper, 156, 164, 165
Lange, Engineer, 140
Leiter, Levi Z., 270
Leopold II, King of Belgium, 193

Liebaw, Richard, 221
Littell's Living Age, 52
Locksteadt, Chas. F., 163
London, electric lighting of, 188
London Engineering, 77, 135
Lowrey, Grosvenor P., 165

MACALPINE, JOHN H., 185
McClain, Samuel, 298
MacDonald, Dr. Carlos F., 155
Macfarland, 283
McKinley, William, 284; family in White House, 270
Mallary, Mrs. Raymond, 281
Mascart, Professor E., 174
Master Car Builders' Association, 92
Mather, Robert, 216
Maw, W. H., 77
Melville, Rear-Admiral George W., 185, 271
Meter, an electric current, 140
Miller, John F., 248
Motor, Tesla electric, 141

NEW YORK, the current struggle in, 143
Niagara, from, to the Navy, 171; River power developed, 170; International, Commission, 173; present power plants, 177

O'BRIEN, JUDGE MORGAN J., 200
Oliver, Senator George T., 298
Osborne, Loyall A., 135

PANTALEONI, GUIDO, 134, 138
Parsons, Charles Algernon, 183
Peary, Rear-Admiral Robert E., 298
Philadelphia Company, 124, 197
Pitcairn, Robert, 64, 126
Pittsburgh, what natural gas did for, 119
Pope, Franklin L., 138
Post, George A., 194

RAILWAY, electric button system, 180; International Congress, 194; Manhattan Elevated, system, 181
Railways, third rail system on Street, 182
Ratcliffe, William, 20, 36

Rea, Samuel, 298
Reed, Judge J. H., 207
Rodman, Hugh, 245
Rotary engine idea, 41
Rowland, Prof. Henry A., 174
Ryan, Thomas Fortune, 199

SAGE, RUSSELL, 181
Schiff, Jacob H., 202
Schmid, Albert, 134
Scott, Charles F., 135
Scott, Rev. Walter, 37
Sellers, Dr. Coleman, 173
Shallenberger, Oliver B., 134, 140
Sherman, Roger M., 154
Signalling, experiments in, 102
Sleeth, J. Hunter, 298
Sleeth, Samuel D., 298
Slideometer device, 94
Smith, Frank S., 276
"Solitude", estate at Homewood, 74
Stanley, William, 131
Stewart, James C., 190
Stewart, John A., 202
Stewart, Lorenzo, 32
Stewart, Dr. William A., 284
Stillwell, Lewis B., 135, 174, 281, 283
Straight-air brakes, 88
Switching, experiments in, 102

TATE, DANIEL, 68
Taylor, Frank H., 243, 280
Terry, Charles A., 165, 293
Tesla, Nikola, 134, 139, 244
Thomson, Sir William, 174
Towne, Sup't C. B. & Q. R.R., 50
Townley, Calvert, 275
Turretini, Col. Theodore, 174
Twombley, Hamilton McK., 173

UNDERWOOD, FREDERICK D., 298
Union Switch & Signal Company, 132
Unwin, Prof. William Cawthorne, 174
Uptegraff, Walter D., 207, 293

VACUUM BRAKES, 87, 92
Van der Weyde, Dr. P. H., 147

WELLS, PROF. WILLIAM, 38
Westinghouse Electric Company organization, 139

Westinghouse, George, personal characteristics, 1; birthplace at Central Bridge, N. Y., 1; father and mother, 2, 13, 17, 21, 23, 25, 36, 61, 71, 292; circumstances of his birth, 5; childhood, 10; removal to Schenectady, 13; mechanical tastes, 16; first earnings, 17; ingenuity, 18, 20; education, 19; school and teachers, 22; desire to enter the army, 23, 30; attempt to run away, 25; recruiting services, 32; experience as a soldier, 33; trying the Navy, 35; entering Union College, 37; no taste for languages, 38; a man's wages, 40; returning to mechanical pursuits, 40; invents car replacer, 42; making cast steel railway frogs, 42; meeting with his future wife, 45; marriage, 46; Mont Cenis tunnel experiments, 54; breaking with his partners, 56; moving to Pittsburgh, 58; early discouragements, 62; first real test of the air brake, 69; patenting the air brake, 72; air brake company first organized, 73; goes to England, 74, 76; early progress in Europe, 90; electrical appliances with air brakes, 93; triumphal train tour of the country, 99; Master Car Builders' Association report, 100; interested in natural gas, 106; defending the alternating current, 149; magazine controversy with Thomas A. Edison, 150; controversy over electric death penalty, 153; effective personality, 156; needing a half million dollars, 158; criticized by his creditors, 159; invades money circles in New York, 160; trusted by employees and contractor, 161; detective instinct, 166; highly complimented by the Columbian Exposition, 170; refuses a first offer for advice on Niagara, 174; experiments with electric power on Erie Canal, 176; theories regarding a future gas engine, 180; electrifying street railways, 180; relations with Manhattan Elevated Railway, 181; on the "third rail" system, 182; steam turbine researches, 183; undertaking the electric lighting of London, 188; contracting with James C. Stewart, 190; scholastic degrees and honors for, 193; Grashof medal, 193; John Fritz medal, 194; address before International Railway Congress, 194; complimented by N. Y. *Life*, 196; as trustee for the Equitable Life Assurance Co., 201; second financial ordeal, 204; Electric & Manufacturing Company most seriously involved, 206; omitting annual meeting of his great company, 208; calmness under great distress, 210; collapse as a financier, 217; and the automobile industry, 219; inventing his air spring, 222; as a public speaker, 223; on the Trust question, 224; on industrial standardization, 226; on the ultimate electrification of all railways, 228; prophecies of industrial future of South, 229; on the disciplinary policy of Germany, 231; admired by his employees, 232; stories about, and his employees, 235; benevolence of, 240; habits of working, 241; proposed Alaskan wheat experiment, 242; beginning of his air-brake factory, 246; Thanksgiving dinner custom, 247; Saturday half-holiday custom, 247; workmen's pension system, 248; workmen's relief department, 248; educational work among young employees, 250; care for the girls in his employ, 251; on the labor union question, 253; benevolence to his workmen, 255; hatred of treachery, 258; and his trio of homes, 259; private car, the Glen Eyre, 259; homes at Lenox, Mass., Pittsburgh, Pa., and Washington, D. C., 259; Lenox estate and the electric apparatus for moving water, 269; home on Dupont Circle, Washington, 270; domestic traits, 271; sensitiveness to criticism of his financial failure, 274; positiveness, 276; generosity to inventors, 277; and the rat-trap man, 277; honesty in business, 278; fishing habits, 282; interest in public affairs, 283; admiration for Cleveland, 284; relations with McKinley, 284; on popular government, 285; love of country, 286; dislike of newspaper portraits, 287; best photograph ever taken, 288; hatred of using his name for advertising, 289; "last scene of all", 290; heavy colds, 291; will, 293; breakdown in health, 294; accident in keelless boat, 295; nieces playing tennis, 295; last illness, 296; death, 297; funeral, 297; inscription on tombstone, 299; industrious to the last, 299

Westinghouse, George, Jr., 106, 267; marriage of, 298; Mrs. George, Jr., 298; children, 298

Westinghouse, Henry Herman, 13, 126, 131, 293

Westinghouse, Jay, 14

Westinghouse, John, 14, 23, 29, 30, 34, 36, 293

Westinghouse Machine Company, 131

Westinghouse, Marguerite Erskine Walker, 46, 106, 134; and her "Solitude" estate, 260; helping to lay out her Lenox estate, 263; as a farmer, 267; as the author of diffused electric lighting, 268; handling reception to American Society of Mechanical Engineers, 270; benevolence, 294

Westinghouse Office Building, 128

Whitcomb, G. D., 73

Williams, Edward H., 65, 73

CPSIA information can be obtained
at www.ICGtesting.com
Printed in the USA
FSOW03n0815041116
26979FS